Electronically Speaking:
Computer Speech Generation

John P. Cater—Mr. Cater has a B.S. Electrical Engineering, Texas Tech University and an MBA, Trinity University, Texas. He is presently employed at Southwest Research Institute, San Antonio, Texas as Manager–Intelligent Systems Engineering Section. He is responsible for generation and successful conduct of applied electronics research in digital-RF interface systems. He has had recent experience in digital synthetic speech technology and applications. Mr. Cater presented papers at Computer Faire 80 and 81.

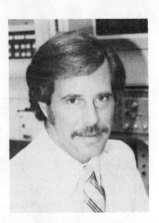

Electronically Speaking: Computer Speech Generation

by

John P. Cater

Howard W. Sams & Co., Inc.
4300 WEST 62ND ST. INDIANAPOLIS, INDIANA 46268 USA

Copyright © 1983 by Howard W. Sams & Co., Inc.
Indianapolis, IN 46268

FIRST EDITION
FIRST PRINTING—1983

International Standard Book Number: 0-672-21947-6
Library of Congress Catalog Card Number: 82-051043

Edited by: *Bob Manville*
Illustrated by: Wm. D. Basham
              T.R. Emrick
              Ron Troxell
Printed in the United States of America.

Preface

As the world continues to develop computers and to model them in man's image, they are given peripherally greater powers of intelligence and senses attributed to the human. Research into computer characteristics such as artificial intelligence, audio and visual response, and other sensory perceptions is occurring at breakneck speeds at computer laboratories around the world. The particular computer characteristic which this book will examine is that of artificial or computer speech as used in large and small computers in today's technology.

The intent of this book is to give you a better understanding of the techniques and principles used for generating synthetic speech while not omitting the more practical but mundane considerations of the implications of synthetic speech in today's already computer conscious society. Most references to computer speech, to date, have included only the "nuts and bolts" of generating computer speech without guidance as to the pitfalls and cautions to be avoided when applying synthetically generated speech. These admonitions are often obvious after a system has been designed, developed, and put into practical use. But, in many cases, they are realized too late in the introductory cycle of a product or system for changes to be implemented; and the concept is doomed to failure.

Contained within this book is a brief introduction to the elements of human speech from a physiological or biomechanical standpoint, and a short crash course on our tools for speaking:

Linguistics. After these basic elements of the natural human process called speaking are understood, we will delve into the techniques currently used for generating nonhuman speech and the available products on today's market for implementing the synthesized speech peripheral on small computers.

The first chapter is an introduction to computer generated speech, designed primarily for the novice who is interested in learning at a glance what the current technological upheaval in computer generated synthetic speech is all about. This chapter will give you the basic fundamentals of computer speech and bring you quickly up to date so that you can more easily understand the technology for new synthetic speech applications.

The second chapter presents the physical aspects of speech and how we humans do it. While this chapter is rather biological, its concepts should be understood in order to adequately comprehend the methods and techniques described in later chapters. Since the intent of the synthetic speech peripheral is to model human speech, a cursory understanding of human speech mechanics illustrates the enormity of the task of creating the same sounds from a string of ones and zeros.

Chapter three is like an operating manual for the human or computer mouth. The mechanics of speech described in Chapter Two are useless without some rules by which to speak. In this case, the English language is featured. The field of linguistics presented in this chapter is closely akin to that subject you hated in school. However, now that it applies to your computer, pay attention! This is one of the more important aspects of computer speech. Its fundamentals must be understood before you can properly transfer your knowledge of speech to your computer. If you skip this chapter, don't expect your computer to sound like Dan Rather on the evening news. The results of your technical efforts to generate synthetic speech without a basic knowledge of linguistics may sound more like Andy Koffmann or Donald Duck. In other words, you are presented in this chapter with the "software" for creating speech from the talking mechanism. Without a grasp of this knowledge, you are essentially trying to program a computer without software.

Chapter Four breaks away from the technical content of this book for a brief glimpse at some rather important etiquette rules for implementing a talking computer. If your reason for reading this book is to create a computer system that talks to people, it should be expected to observe certain speech etiquette rules which are often neglected by both humans and computers. Reading of this chapter may be delayed, if you desire, until the novelty of your synthetic speech system wears off. It is a must when you begin to say "Shut-up Computer." This is not a frivolous chapter. It presents common sense considerations that should be included in the design of talking computers from speaking home-burglar alarms to babbling electronic games.

The fifth chapter brings you quickly up to date on the history of research into synthesized speech. This chapter is presented primarily because of the old adage that if we do not know the past, then we are doomed to repeat it. Besides that, it's rather interesting to see how far the technology of teaching a machine to talk has come in the past 100 years. (And that's about how long ago it started.)

Chapter Six plunges headlong into the technical description of current speech synthesis technology. Each of the foremost technologies for creating artificial speech is presented and described in detail. This chapter begins by describing waveform coding of speech, proceeds through analog formant synthesis methods, linear predictive coding (LPC) speech for precoded and phonetic systems, partial autocorrelation (PARCOR) methods, and ends with a description of fringe techniques which are currently being researched and will most likely appear in the future when the hardware technology permits.

The seventh chapter is a review of the available off-the-shelf speech synthesis peripherals for small computers. Each manufacturer's product is categorized as to the type of speech generation technology utilized. A brief review of each system's theory of operation is given so that you may better decide which of these devices best suits your own computer needs.

The eighth chapter presents a potpourri of synthetic speech applications from those existing in today's marketplace to those you may be the first to implement on your own home computer. This chapter has some blue sky information on future speech applications based on current corporate research directions. No matter which speech peripheral device you have chosen, you will invariably find an application in this compendium of real world uses to tickle your fancy.

At the end of the book, you will find a list of reference reading materials which may guide you in more detail to the particular area of your interests. Be forewarned that much of this material is rather heavy reading and not designed for casual perusal.

Finally, a glossary of terms relating to the field of computer generated synthetic speech is included in the event you run across a word in this book that you never have seen before. It also provides a rather comprehensive dictionary for reading other technical literature relating to the field of computer generated synthetic speech.

JOHN P. CATER

To my dear wife Jaye, who patiently slept through the writing of this book.

Contents

CHAPTER 1

INTRODUCTION TO COMPUTER SPEECH SYNTHESIS 11
Tell Me What's Happening!—What Said That?

CHAPTER 2

PHYSIOLOGICALLY SPEAKING: HOW DO WE DO IT? 21
Say "Hello"—Cerebral Cogitation—The Ears Have It—
Hearing Theories—The Human Speech Output Mechanism

CHAPTER 3

A WORD ON LINGUISTICS 41
Say Aaahhh—The Vowel Sounds—The Other Sounds:
Consonants—Onward and Upward—This Is a Test—A Final
Word on Linguistics

CHAPTER 4

COMPUTER SPEECH ETIQUETTE 58
Cater's Laws of Computer Speech—Obey the Law!—Now
Can I Say It?—Get Smarter—Minimal Considerations—
Freedom of Speech?

CHAPTER 5

SPEECH SYNTHESIS: AN HISTORICAL REVIEW 71
Talking Mechanisms—Into the 20th Century

CHAPTER 6

A CLOSER LOOK AT TODAY'S TECHNIQUES 79
The Trinity of Speech Technology—Computer Synthetic
Speech—The Waveform Encoding/Reconstruction Tech-
nique—Analog Formant Frequency Speech Synthesis—
Analog Formant Speech Frequency Synthesizers—Linear
Predictive Coded (LPC) Speech—Fringe Techniques

CHAPTER 7

OFF-THE-SHELF SPEECH SYNTHESIS SYSTEMS 121
Waveform Encoded/Reconstructed Systems—Analog Formant Speech Synthesizers—Digital Vocal Tract Modeling Synthesizers

CHAPTER 8

A COMPUTER SPEECH POTPOURRI 179
The Minimal System—The Talking Home Computer With
Peripherals—Commercial Applications of Synthetic Speech

APPENDIX A

GLOSSARY OF TERMS 199

APPENDIX B

ADVANCED READINGS 213

APPENDIX C

SPEECH SYNTHESIS PRODUCT MANUFACTURERS 215

APPENDIX D

SPEECH SYNTHESIS APPLICATIONS CIRCUIT COLLECTION ... 217
INDEX 227

chapter 1

Introduction to Computer Speech Synthesis

The task of writing an introduction for a book on electronic speech synthesis must be likened to the problem that Christopher Columbus had when he first sat down to describe his trip to the new world in 1492. As you delve deeper into the pages of this book, you will find yourself on a fantastic journey into the body and mind of man traveling through a land where science fact and science fiction coexist. Only a few short years ago science fiction writers conjured up powerful computer systems and robots which had the capability of voice output. Now, less than a generation later, science technology has extended itself to encompass the realm of those futuristic prophets. Not only has the technology for generating speech from computers left the research laboratories, it is available to you for use with your home computing system.

The reason that this book on computer synthetic speech may be considered a scientific voyage into man is that, for the first time, science has attempted to duplicate a physiological process. Synthetic speech scientists could not simply sit down with equations and slide rules or calculators and decide how to create speech from electronic machines. Instead, they had to understand the mechanics of speech as we humans utter it, and then formulate electronic equivalents for simulating the vocal tract. Can you imagine the difficulty that the first computer scientists might have had if they had attempted to model the digital computer from the gray matter within our heads? Had that occurred, then computers as we know them today might be chemical in origin rather than electronic.

Of course, this may still come to pass as man begins to relate his science technology to living counterparts, but the understanding of the human speech mechanism is many, many times less complex than that of the brain. In keeping with the original learning process, the chapters of this book will introduce you to some of the physiological aspects of speech and the associated thought processes that create what we refer to as spoken communications. Then, after a short chapter on the history of talking machine research, you will find yourself racing through today's and tomorrow's technology for generating synthetic speech. There is also a chapter for those of you who are not really interested in the mechanisms of computer generated synthetic speech but are just looking for a review of up-to-date speech products.

Travelers on the trip are not required to be scientists. While I do assume that you know something about computers, the pages of this book are written for the neophyte to speech synthesis as well as the professional. Basic concepts are explained in simple terms for ease of understanding. These evolve into more complex ideas as you continue. When you complete this scientific odyssey into computer speech technology you will have arrived at tomorrow's new world.

Tell Me What's Happening!

From the beginning, eons ago when man began to utter his first sounds, he accepted verbal communication as a part of life. We now go from day to day, on our merry way, using speech as a means of acknowledgment, communications, or information transfer. Fortunately, we are required to give very little conscious thought to the process of generating speech. Otherwise, we might have to stop what we are doing to communicate verbally. And, since verbal communication is one of the most efficient means that we possess to express our thoughts and feelings, we use it freely. In fact, it would not be unrealistic to say that each of us speaks on the average of 40,000 words per day. Can you imagine that in writing? A transcription of one person's speech throughout his life would fill libraries. So, without further belaboring the subject, it appears that spoken output is one of our most necessary and useful forms of communication. Remember, however, that in most cases, verbal communication is very temporary, existing only in echoes and your memory after the message has been spoken. On the other hand, written communication is considered to be a permanent record of thought processes.

With the advent of the electronic computing machine in the 1900s, man began to realize that he had created a device with the capability for intelligent response to his commands. Using the technologies available at the time, the electronic computer was first made to infer its outputs through blinking lights, then later with printed messages. Although the first computers chugged along, printing their messages at 60 words per minute, improvements continued. Man's quest for knowledge and product improvement has put at our disposal, with today's technology, the laser page printer which produces its written output at up to 600 pages per minute. Imagine, if you can, a computer outputting data at a rate approaching ten pages per second. Over a single day period, this computer can produce almost a million pages of information!

In parallel with the development of the computer, other scientists were creating electronic vocal tract simulators that could artificially generate the human voice. Their efforts in these areas did not revolve around the computer, but rather consisted primarily of human control. As the two technologies matured, a cross fertilization occurred. The computer began to speak. The first few feeble spoken words from the computer were considered a novelty of human egocentricity. The computer was, in fact, beginning to be modeled in man's image. We have since learned, however, that a computer capability for direct human interaction (in terms of speech output and input) is quite convenient and normal for us. This field has recently attracted the attention of the electronic industry. It has become a burgeoning field while still in its infancy.

The contents of this book describe the background and technology of today's computer generated synthetic speech. These are the technologies as they exist in the 1980s. Since man's capability for understanding complexity seems to double every five years, it's very possible that they might be archaic in the 1990s. But we have to start somewhere. We begin to walk by crawling. Then we learn to run. Our capabilities for artificial speech generation lie somewhere between crawling and walking at the current time. These consist of three basic forms, each technologically different:

1. the waveform encoding/reconstruction technique,
2. the analog formant frequency synthesis technique,
3. the digital vocal tract modeling of speech.

The waveform encoding/reconstruction of speech is one of the most basic and elementary forms of making a computer talk. Operationally, the computer becomes, in effect, a simple voice recorder. The computer, in this case, uses its digital memory rather than magnetic tape or phonograph record grooves for storage. The desired output phrases and words are stored as response units and then "played back" by the applications program as needed. The capability for generating a word that has not been "prestored" in memory does not exist. This system requires very little additional computer hardware to create a spoken output. But, there is a fatal flaw. The storage of direct waveform encoded speech in memory requires considerable space. While the fidelity of the spoken output can approach a very high quality recording, the memory requirements for the message can be overwhelming.

However, if the vocabulary requirements are not excessively large (under 10 or 15 words or phrases), then this method becomes a viable and inexpensive technique. Fig. 1-1 shows the essentials of the waveform encoding/synthesis technique. Its

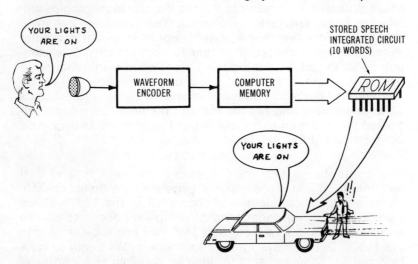

Fig. 1-1. Waveform encoding synthesis.

use in fixed vocabulary applications such as the talking automobile control panel is quite natural. Since the appropriate messages to be spoken are all predetermined, based on the automobile's status, they can be stored in a limited memory space. This allows a rather compact and inexpensive voice output for the automobile dashboard.

The second speech synthesis technique is the formant frequency synthesis method. This voice synthesizer, which is fundamentally different from the previous one, is typically rather unnatural in its sound because of the means of excitation. The robotic sound from the formant synthesizer stems from the lack of direct human speech input for a resultant spoken message. In other words, speech synthesized by a formant synthesizer is truly originated by the computer. The principles behind the formant synthesizer described in more detail throughout this book are based on the acoustic replication of the human vocal tract. Bandpass filters are used to create formant frequencies characteristic of human speech. The sum of the formant filters closely resembles the frequency spectrum of speech and therefore is interpreted by our ears as a verbal message.

An advantageous flexibility of the formant frequency method of speech synthesis is the inherent unlimited vocabulary capability. Since speech is generated by the recreation of speech sounds, any word can be spoken by correctly piecing together the sounds to be spoken. This flexibility, however, comes with the price of intelligibility. The formant synthesizer is not easily understood in many situations. In addition, the great number of English language exceptions between text and spoken words creates problems with producing the unlimited vocabulary.

The most common method for exciting the formant frequency synthesizer is through the use of numerous indentifiable speech sounds called phonemes ('fō-,nēm). By stringing together the correct phonemes in the correct order, based upon the way we speak, the phoneme synthesizer will closely replicate our speech. The mechanism by which this occurs is illustrated in Fig. 1-2. Of course, this extremely simplistic view of formant synthesis ignores the complexities of the actual speech generation. The diagram does show, however, the characteristics of a typical formant synthesizer configuration.

The phoneme-driven formant synthesizer has an advantage in a home computer system in that any word that can be phoneti-

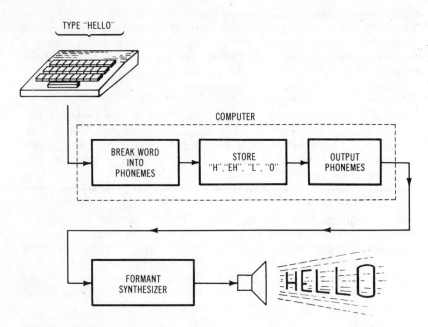

Fig. 1-2. Formant frequency synthesis.

cally described can be phonetically spoken. As a peripheral for a home computer, the output vocabulary is not dependent upon the words that a manufacturer chooses to place in memory. While this might not seem important to you at first, consider how many manufacturers might put, for instance, your own name into a preencoded vocabulary. None! This illustrates the flexibility of the formant synthesizer. Although the same capability exists within any phoneme-driven synthesizer (there are also LPC phoneme synthesizers), you will not have the luxury of an unlimited vocabulary with any other synthesis method.

The third primary type of speech synthesis can best be described as a digital modeling of the human vocal tract. The most prevalent application of this technique is referred to as linear predictive coded (LPC) speech. Other methods exist which closely resemble LPC speech and are referred to as partial autocorrelation (PARCOR) and parametric waveform encoding of speech. All of these synthesis methods are highly mathematical in their operation because they simulate the actions of the human vocal tract with equations. Since the human vocal tract is a rather complex acoustic system, the equations are also necessarily complex.

16

The advantages of the digital vocal tract simulators are the ease of implementation on a digital integrated circuit, a subsequent lower production cost, and a lower data rate. The vocabulary for this type of synthesizer is typically generated by a human speaker like the waveform encoding synthesis method. However, rather than directly storing the speech as sampled information, the digital vocal tract simulation methods separate human speech into its various frequencies and vocal characteristics. This speech dissection greatly decreases the amount of storage required for spoken output. This is one of the major advantages of this method of speech synthesis. An immediately apparent example of the advantages of this method is visible in the Speak and Spell™* children's learning aid manufactured by Texas Instruments. This relatively inexpensive device has the capability for about 200 words of truly synthesized LPC speech. The computer which drives the synthesizer is actually within the Speak and Spell, and consists of a 4-bit microprocessor. The children's learning toy has over the past few years been followed by many other similar speaking hand-held devices. While talking toys are not exactly new (dolls and telephones have used miniature phonographs for years), the use of direct speech synthesis within toys provides for highly intelligible speech and a much higher mechanical reliability.

The mechanism by which digital vocal tract modeling works is represented in Fig. 1-3. Although the appearance of the synthesis process is very similar to the waveform encoding synthesis method, the primary difference lies in the amount of speech storage available for the same memory. This is also accompanied by a very slight difference in speech quality, hardly noticeable to the average listener. The result of this storage efficiency is, of course, a lower cost per stored word in the final product. As larger and larger vocabularies are needed for marketed products, the advantages of digital vocal tract modeling will surely be exploited.

What Said That?

The applications for speech synthesis in today's products are endless. If we look at some of the basic requirements, we see the people that can best use the spoken output are those handicapped by poor sight or loss of vision entirely. For them,

---

*Speak and Spell is a trademark of Texas Instruments, Inc.

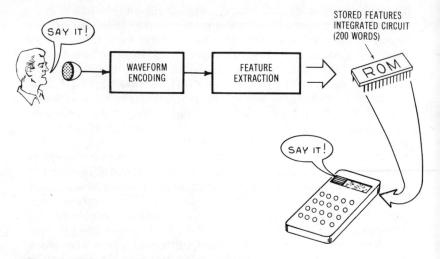

Fig. 1-3. Digital vocal tract modeling synthesis.

a speaking machine gives them the use of a new product in which Braille was impractical. Along this line, the talking reading machine has become invaluable. Using the technology of optical character recognition combined with unlimited vocabulary synthesis, unsighted people no longer need the help of a human reader to pursue literary interests. While these reading machines are still in their first generation, they have proved to be a boon for the unsighted individual.

As another pertinent application of speech synthesis to the handicapped, consider those who lack the ability to speak. All of their previous methods of communication with other persons have been limited to either sign language or written messages. The development of a speaking machine with a keyboard for generating speech allows them to speak with an artificial voice almost as easily as they can point at a word. Although the cost of these machines is relatively high for current products, the beehive of activity in the speech synthesis market will surely create low-cost competitors in future markets.

If we turn our attention away from the essential uses of speech synthesis to ones which might be considered optional, we still find some very appropriate applications. As you fly from place to place on those luxury jets in the sky, there is, within the avionics of the cockpit, a synthetic voice waiting to warn the pilot and copilot of impending emergencies. If you stop to consider the number of dials and meters that these airline pilots must monitor, you can see how they might miss the illuminiation of a small lamp to indicate an engine fire. So, in an effort to simplify their information overload problem while flying, emergency messages for such warnings as engine fires, altitude dangers, and mechanical malfunctions have been delegated to an automatically triggered speech synthesizer. The synthetic voice immediately directs the attention of the crew to the danger. This is one synthesizer you never want to hear!

Another very practical but optional use of speech synthesis is becoming evident in telephone response systems. Since we are limited to verbal messages (except with data terminals), over telephone lines, a speech synthesizer makes an excellent interface between the human and the computer. By combining the features of the Touch-Tone®* dial with a computer speech synthesizer, machines now exist that automatically quote stock market exchange prices, bank balances, and credit ratings without the need for remote human interaction. As voice technology progresses, the Touch-Tone mechanism will surely be replaced with voice recognition technology. When that time comes, you may have trouble deciding whether you are talking to a person or a computer. Imagine the horror of receiving a junk phone call from a computer that not only talks *but* also listens.

As we continue an overview of the range of speech synthesis applications, we quickly find the novelty uses. These can be easily identified because the use of speech synthesis in those products is almost superfluous to the operation of the device. Although there are some advantages to be found as these appliances and machines begin to speak, the speech capability is placed there primarily because of its novelty. One of the major advantages of placing a speech capability in a home appliance, for instance, is that verbal messages and instructions can be given without the use of a cathode ray tube (crt) indicator or printed message. And, as you would expect, the cost of a speech synthesizer is considerably lower than visual methods of similar output.

No matter how the speech synthesizer is being used commercially, its most important application will be the way that *you*

---

*Touch-Tone is a registered trademark of the American Telephone and Telegraph Co.

prefer to use it with your home computer. If you are presently considering the purchase or construction of a speech synthesizer for your computer, you will inevitably find applications ranging from the novelty uses to essential applications. The chapter in this book relating to applications gives you some possible suggestions for applying your speaking system. These include talking computer games, talking home security systems, and even a complete voice response security lock system. You will find that once you have mastered the art of speech synthesis integration into your computer, you won't seem to have the spare time that you used to have. Giving your home computer the gift of speech is one of the most gratifying and challenging investments that you can make. And, while you're having fun doing it, don't be surprised if you learn a few things you didn't know before.

As we continue our voyage through the world of speech synthesis, our first stop will be the vocal tract. If you are really in a hurry to get to the electronics of speech synthesis, then take an express ride to Chapter 6. Do not, however, discount the next four chapters. They will give you a tremendous insight into the development path of today's speech synthesis technology. They are necessary reading for a full understanding of any speech synthesis system. With that in mind, let's begin our voyage.

chapter   2

Physiologically Speaking: How Do *We* Do It?

Say "Hello"

To begin the chapter on biomechanical aspects of speaking, let's attempt a simple experiment. Open your mouth and say "hello." That wasn't too difficult was it? As a matter of fact, you most likely didn't really have to think about it to create the process that we call "speech."

In the remainder of this chapter, we will examine and analyze the processes that occurred while you formulated the word "hello" and transferred it (via your central nervous system) to the various muscles of your body to generate speech. We'll also look at how you simultaneously monitored the progression of the expected vocal envelope with your ears to keep the word sounding like your "vocal memory." Of course, your first impression may be to think that the task of speaking such a simple word requires very little attention from the biological and biomechanical processes within your body. If this were the case, then the generation of synthetic speech would be a rather elementary task. As we delve deeper into the process of creating a single word of speech, we will begin to see the intricacies of the speech process that we take for granted in the human. Only then can we better understand the difficulties in creating artificial speech.

Cerebral Cogitation

The basis for the spoken word "hello" in the previous simplistic experiment originated in your brain as a thought. In this specific case, the thought was keyed to the sight of the recognizable printed word "hello." The neurological messages from your eyes traveled through the optical nerves to your brain. The brain then quickly performed a vocabulary search through your resident vocal vocabulary, found "hello," and produced the parameters for speech. A rather simplified illustration of the physiological speech network which contains the visual input link is shown in Fig. 2-1. This anatomical drawing provides a view, for illustration purposes, of the input and output links from the brain which serve as the organs of human speech. Now let's examine them in more detail.

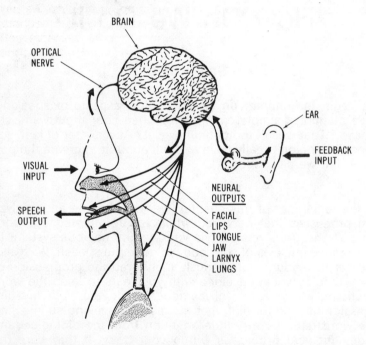

Fig. 2-1. Simplified physiological speech network.

The method by which the visual signals travel from the optical nerves in the eye to the brain is through the optical nerve link. One of the more interesting features of this link is that it is a direct link with the brain, bypassing the spinal cord over which the remainder of the brain's input and output signals pass. Not only does this prevent the confusion of visual signals with those passing to other parts of the body, it also provides the closest path of connection for almost immediate visual response. If this were not so, your reaction time to visual inputs would be greatly extended due to the travel time of the neurons' signals through the central nervous system.

As we search the intricacies of the brain and nervous system, we must have at least a casual understanding of the interconnecting "wires" that feed the signals to and from the various input and output "peripherals." In the case of the human body, the wires and their associated cabling are called the nervous system. Now you may ask, how can living organisms be considered wires? Well, take a moment to consider that the electrical conductivity process within a copper wire consists of little more than electrons passing from one copper atom to the next in a rather torrential flow. From the atomic view it becomes somewhat easier to understand how a bundle of nerve cells called neurons can pass electrochemical signals throughout the body in small fractions of a second.

The miniscule neurons (the human body contains approximately fifteen billion) are made up of microscopic masses of protoplasm enclosed in rather porous membranes or sheaths. For the sake of simplicity, let's consider protoplasm in this description as the most basic constituent of the living cell. Since the intent of this book is not to review the basics of biology, we will assume that neurons are, in effect, the connecting conductors that carry the brain's input and output signals throughout the human body. The method by which the signal is passed through the living cells is similar to the galvanic action that occurs within the rechargeable battery. In other words, if the chemicals nickel and cadmium were combined with their oxides into a chemical combination, the system would be capable of holding an electrical charge. In a like process, the neurons in the nervous system can pass electrical charges from the brain to the various nerve endings.

At the end of each nerve bundle are input/output cells referred to as either receptor cells or effector cells. The receptor cells in the eyes and ears act as the television camera and microphone for visual and aural inputs. These sensors send their signals through the neurons of the nervous system to the brain where neural activity continues in the form of memory searches. As the referenced information stored in the brain's neurons is accessed, a varitable flood of data is retrieved for subsequent use by the recognition and motor centers of the brain. You can most easily understand this sequence if you remember, during the experiment, reading the word "hello" *before* trying to speak it. You probably recognized that it was a casual greeting spoken between friends or strangers at first sight. It also possibly created a sense of friendliness and well being. As these almost subconscious thoughts were occurring within your mind, there was a simultaneous process occurring to retrieve the imbedded motor control information to create speech in the form of the verbal word "hello." As we shall see later in this chapter, the physical control of the approximately 50 muscles required for speech generation during that word (containing approximately five basic phonetic sounds) would require at least 250 accesses of your prestored vocabulary word "hello." If you consider further that a transition from one sound to another requires smoothly changing muscle configurations within the face, the complexity of the task grows. The final interaction which must be considered during the spoken experiment is the aural feedback from the auditory system or ears. Thus, the brain continuously monitors the progress of the vocal cords and sound modification processes occurring within the mouth and throat to correctly speak the word as remembered.

The Ears Have It

Your first inclination upon seeing this topic in a chapter on human speech may be to ask "what does the ear have to do with the speech process?" If you really have trouble believing that this effect is of paramount importance to proper and articulate speech, then let me suggest another rather simple experiment which may convince you on this point. Take an inexpensive audio cassette recorder with a microphone and find yourself a rather comfortable sentence from any text within this book. Then read the sentence aloud while recording your voice. The second part of the experiment, now that you have made a reference recording, will involve recording the same sentence aloud while your hearing has been artifically impaired. This effect may be accomplished in a number of ways. Some rather simple means of temporarily impairing your hearing are to simply plug your ears with your fingers or put on a set of stereo headphones with the volume loud enough to overshadow your own speech. Another method is having another person talk very closely into your ears while you are attempting to repeat the same sentence. None of these methods will provide the simulation of a complete loss of hearing because of the bone conduction feedback that still exists within your face. However, after having tried recording the sentence twice under the two conditions, you should notice the slight difference in your speech pattern, due only to the lack of auditory feedback during the speech process.

The most startling effect which can illustrate the primary importance of audio feedback in generating proper speech patterns is the use of an audio delay line or echo chamber fed to headphones from the recording microphone. If you have ever tried this experiment at a science fair or have spoken over the pa system in a large auditorium, then you should have noticed that audio feedback from your *delayed* speech is worse than no feedback at all. The most accurate description of the sounds which are generated during delayed audio feedback speech are very chopped and almost stutter-like in quality.

A more passive way to perform the previous experiment is to observe the speech patterns of people around you with hearing disabilities or defects. You will most likely notice some commonalities among their vocal outputs. The most common disturbance in their speech pattern is a louder than normal amplitude, sometimes to the point of shouting. They are not talking louder than normal to request you to do the same thing, but rather to increase the level of their speech feedback. Another trait which may be noticed is that the sounds made with the lips and the teeth (fricative and plosive sounds) are in a different proportion to the voiced sounds such as vowels made by a person with normal hearing. This effect results from the low pass filter mechanism of the bones in the face, providing aural feedback of the low frequency component voiced sounds. These vibrations are passed to the auditory system in greater amplitude than the higher frequency fricative and plosive sounds such as *F, P, T, K, S, Z,* and *CH.* If the hearing loss has a uniform frequency attenuation, then the speech will have a normal proportion of high frequency and low frequency sounds but be somewhat louder than normal conversation. As the hearing loss becomes more severe, the feedback of the higher frequencies (as previously mentioned) disappears, creating a disproportion of speech sounds in the high frequency and low frequency range. A further discussion of these sounds and their frequency components is given in Chapter 3.

So, if we now concede that the ear does play a very important role in the production of articulate human speech, let's take a brief look at its capabilities. The ear is a marvelous piece of instrumentation simulating a microphone to the brain, but providing a dynamic range or range of amplitude hearing that surpasses almost any electronic system available.

The frequency range of the normal human ear is from approximately 15 Hz to about 20,000 Hz. This range, however, is time variant with a progressively decreasing frequency range with age at the higher end of the audio spectrum. While young children may have a high frequency response extending to possibly 30,000 Hz, the hardening of the aging eardrum and associated inner ear organs causes a drop off in the high frequency response to between 10,000 and 15,000 Hz. Fortunately, since the highest frequency component of human speech used for aural feedback is approximately 6,000 to 8,000 Hz, normal speech generation is not affected by this aging process.

Hearing Theories

There have been several theories developed by medical scientists throughout the ages as to how the ear converts the impending sound waves to physiological signals for the brain. The first, proposed by Herman Von Helmholtz, a rather prominent German scientist in the middle 1800s, suggested that the ear consisted of a number of tuned filaments like the strings of a harp to resonate with incoming audio frequencies. This was like assuming that the ear consisted of a large number of tuned filters with acoustic transducers attached to each discrete frequency filter for sorting out by the mind. This theory has been named the *resonance theory* of hearing.

A second theory formulated in the early 1900s is named the *telephone theory*. This theory assumed that the eardrum and associated organs converted sound waves to electrical impulses exactly like a microphone converts sound waves to electrical signals. The theory went on to assume that the nerves carried signals from the eardrums to the brain like the wires from a microphone to an amplifier. Then, all signal processing was performed within the central nervous system and brain complex. The reason, of course, that this theory was named the telephone theory is that the proposition assumed the method of hearing was exactly like the telephone receiver and microphone (which at that time was a very logical concept).

The final theory, developed in this century, is probably the most correct theory of hearing. It is called the *place theory*. This modern view of hearing is based upon the capability of the ear to distinguish between frequencies as in the resonance theory, but not with tuned resonators. The frequency discrimination comes, instead, from the area or *place* of vibration within the semicircular canals, or cochlea, of the ear as shown in Fig. 2-2. The frequency related signals detected by the receptor nerve cells in the inner ear are then fed through the acoustic nerves to the brain in a parallel-serial combination where signal recognition and analysis occurs.

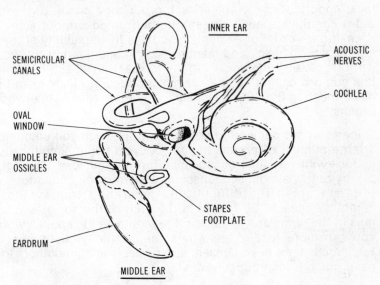

Fig. 2-2. The middle- and inner-ear.

A simplified view of how the proposed theory works is that the perception of tone or pitch is dependent on *which* nerve fibers carry the impulses to the brain in a parallel manner. Volume or loudness, on the other hand, is dependent upon the *number* of impulses along each frequency dependent nerve fiber. Thus, we hear by sensing the amplitude of a number of frequencies simultaneously, with amplitude descriptions at each individual frequency rather than the overall spectrum level. In other words, our hearing system is much like a highly tuned spectrum analyzer with the capability of determining the specific amplitudes of frequencies across the audio spectrum. This not only agrees with the physical structure of the ear, but also accounts for the human capability to detect a 3 Hz change in a pure audio tone of 500 to 1000 Hz (a frequency deviation less than 1%!).

The Human Speech Output Mechanism

SPEECH PRODUCTION

This chapter, to this point, has attempted to provide you with some basic information on how the body perceives and generates the signals to command speech output. After the brain has detected the speech generation signal, analyzed it, and formulated the instruction codes for the vocal system to follow, the production of audible speech may begin. This obviously is the most important link in the speech production chain. But, without it cognitive speech can still be performed without actually speaking a word. For example, you have the capability of reading the word "hello" and mentally saying and hearing the word without causing the vocal organs to react. In effect, by doing this you are calling up the speech production mechanism but disconnecting the output signals to the numerous human vocal organs.

Once you have decided to speak the word, then you command a large number of organs in your body to begin simultaneous actions with very little conscious effort on your part. The complexity of this almost subconscious task must be understood in order to grasp the difficulty in generating true synthetic computer speech. By following the path of the voice as it begins in the lungs and exits from the mouth as the spoken word, you can more readily see why some of the synthetic speech techniques have been chosen, and possibly imagine others that have not yet been conceived.

FROM THE LUNGS TO THE LIPS

The speech generating organs, which are necessary to produce human speech, form a complex hollow tube extending from your lungs to the tips of your lips. The tube (having a total length of approximately one foot) is shown from a side view in Fig. 2-3 along with the remainder of the vocal organs. To understand the flow of speech from the first formation to the final production, you must follow the diagram from the lungs through the windpipe to the larynx, through the throat or pharynx, and finally out the nose and mouth. Although the length of the total cavity is approximately one foot, only in the last six inches or so does the voice actually begin to take shape. Finally, through modification and articulation in the nasal cavities, throat, and mouth, the sound begins to take the form of a recognizable spoken word.

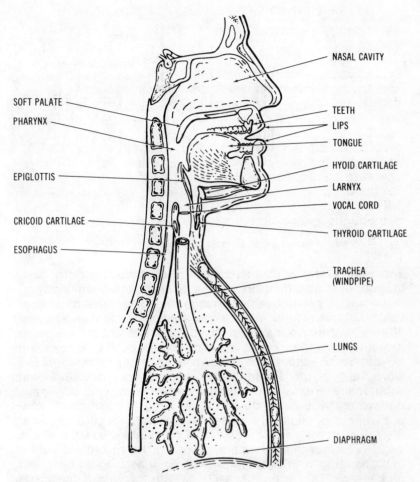

Fig. 2-3. The speech generation organs.

Now, unless you are a third year medical student, the previous anatomical diagram gave you very little information about how the vocal tract acts to produce speech. However, if you use the anatomical drawing in the previous figure with the representative speech mechanism given in Fig. 2-4, you may begin to relate the various functions of the vocal tract with the associated speech effects. A one-to-one correspondence between the figures exists below the mouth because there is very little sound modification occurring in that region. Once the sound or air generated by the lungs and vocal cords passes through the pharynx into the mouth, the analogy becomes more complex.

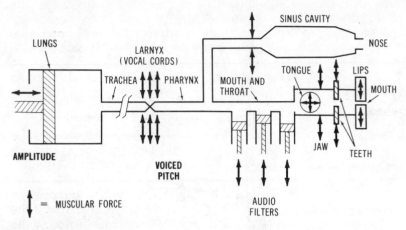

Fig. 2-4. A mechanical view of speech generation.

You may easily confirm this by holding your mouth, jaw, tongue, lips, and teeth in a fixed open position while saying "ah." Now, try to noticeably change the characteristics of your voice without moving any of the previously mentioned vocal "filters" within your mouth. If you did not cheat and move something, the only effect you should have been able to create in your vocal output was either a change in the pitch of the word "ah" or the amplitude (volume) of your output. If you were really creative during that experiment, you may have noticed that you could do one other thing to your speech output without breaking the rules. This change, occurring below the throat in the vocal cords, is the complete relaxation of the vocal cord muscles; therefore, stopping the voiced oscillation and changing your output from voiced speech to an unvoiced air passage. This form of speech, as with the voiced speech, is as important to normal speaking as is the oscillatory sound created by vibrating vocal cords. Later in this chapter we will examine the white noise effect created by simply passing air from the lungs to the vocal tract. First, however, let us examine the operation of the vocal tract and try to find electronic analogies to each interaction as we attempt to understand what we must do electronically to create synthetic human speech.

The first action you must take to begin generating speech is the exhalation of air from the lungs, creating an air flow through the vocal passage. This process occurs any time you breathe through your mouth, but the sound is not audible until you call the vocal organs into action. Once you have decided that the exhalation will become speech, you begin the creation of sound. You can do this by either causing your vocal cords (the larynx) to vibrate or by restricting the air flow with your tongue, teeth, and lips. The choice of these actions creates either the voiced sounds such as vowels, or the fricative sounds such as "S" or "F."

Now suppose that we want to create a word of voiced speech. A good test word which requires no fricative or unvoiced sounds is the exclamation "ow." As we begin to speak the word, consider the sequence of events which must happen.

The lungs begin exhalation of air in a sufficient quantity to create the voluntary vibration of the vocal cords or larynx. If the amount of air generated by the lungs is insufficient to allow the vocal cords to vibrate, then the spoken utterance becomes a whisper. In other words, there is a threshold quantity of air required to cause the vocal cords to begin vibration. You subconsciously decide the correct amount of air before you begin speaking, determined by the volume or amplitude at which you wish to speak. If you try to speak the word very, very softly, you should notice that you may do so by raising the pitch of your voice, but if you try to speak with the same amplitude in a much lower voice, you have to significantly increase the amount of air passing over your vocal cords.

The oscillatory waveform or sound vibration created by the vocal cords resembles the waveform in Fig. 2-5. If you could place a microphone in your throat right above your vocal cords, this would be the waveform you could expect to see on a high

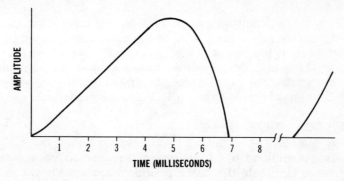

Fig. 2-5. The glottal pulse shape.

gain oscilloscope. The same signal applied to a frequency analysis system or spectrum analyzer would yield the spectrum shown in Fig. 2-6. What this figure means, if you are unfamiliar with the output of a spectral analysis system, is that the glottal pulse shown in Fig. 2-5 has frequency components spread across the audio spectrum. The distribution of these components, however, is highly tilted toward the lower frequencies around 200 to 300 Hz.

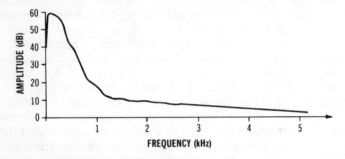

Fig. 2-6. The glottal pulse frequency spectrum.

As the vocal cord muscles are tightened during speech, the fundamental frequency, or primary frequencies, of this distribution curve will rise in frequency to produce a rising change in voice pitch. Typical pitch frequencies for male voices range from 130 Hz to 146 Hz with an average frequency of around 141 Hz. The voice pitch of a female, on the other hand, has a range of approximately 188 Hz to 295 Hz with a median frequency of approximately 233 Hz. Under certain extremes of voice frequency extension during very inflective speech, the human glottal oscillation may reach a pitch as high as 480 Hz.

Now remember that the frequencies we are discussing in relation to the speaking voice are not the overtones created by the resonances of the throat, nose, and mouth, but rather the fundamental frequencies generated by the vocal chord oscillation. In other words, the glottal pulse shown in Fig. 2-5 is repeated at a pitch interval corresponding to these frequencies.

THE VOCAL FILTERS

We have examined the functions of the human vocal system that serve to create the basic sound of speech known as the glottal vibration. Electronic synthesis of the voice to this point is relatively simple because the somewhat simplistic curve of the vocal cord vibration can be stored in electronic memory and later reproduced to create the same basic speech sound.

The most complex part of speech occurs above the vocal cords. The mouth, nose, and lips produce harmonic or overtone filtering to selectively create frequency spectra which fit the recognized sounds we refer to as normal speech patterns. Electronically, this is not simple. In fact, if you will refer back to Fig. 2-4, you will notice that there are a considerable number of movable or adjustable elements in the mouth and throat. Even this simplification does not realistically illustrate the number of audio filters that are present within the oral cavities.

In an earlier section of this chapter we discussed the process of speaking and how the brain generates the signals for speech. These signals eventually command the muscles of the face to begin the audio filtering. If we consider electrical analogies to this process, the computer must command a similar number of filters to very closely approximate the normal expected human speech. If you consider that there are approximately 49 muscles in the face, mouth, and throat that can be moved to modify the previously described glottal pulse, the task of simulating 49 computer-controlled filters becomes rather difficult to imagine. Very few people would attempt to construct 49 audio filters and string them together, much less determine the computer-controlled programming to correctly modify these filters during a spoken utterance. This is the crux of the voice synthesis complication. How do we bring such a complicated mechanism into a form that we can more easily understand and work with?

First, let us examine what happens when a waveform similar to the glottal pulse is injected into an audio filter, whether electronic or acoustic (also known as a resonator). The response of a resonator to an input pulse resembling the glottal pulse shown earlier might be like that given in Fig. 2-7. Even though the upper waveform in this figure has a rather slow period on the order of 100 to 300 Hz, the resonated output from the audio filter "rings" like a struck bell at a frequency four to five times higher than the original input signal. This ringing of the audio filter or resonator is characteristic of any mechanism that tends to resonate. As an illustration, remember when you were a kid and used to blow air across the top of a soda pop bottle to create various tones. As you drank more of the pop, the pitch would lower in frequency. What you were doing during this

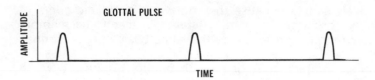

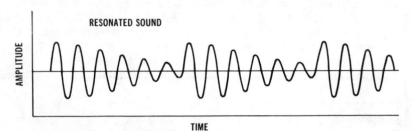

Fig. 2-7. The audio filtering process.

process was changing the length of the resonator within the bottle and, in effect, changing the frequency of the audio filter by changing its shape. This mechanism is very similar to that which occurs within your mouth during the production of overtones from the glottal pulse. Although we have been discussing a single frequency resonator, there are many effective resonators which exist within your vocal tract. Each of these filters has its corresponding resonance frequency (depending upon its shape) which will vary rapidly during speech.

The various resonance frequencies of the cavities within your vocal tract are known as the *formant* frequencies. The formant frequencies, of which three to four are normally required for adequate speech synthesis, may range in frequency from 200 Hz for the first formant in the male speaker to 2000 Hz for the third formant in the female speaker. The exact placement of the formant frequencies within the audio spectrum determines the sound that you interpet as speech. To complicate matters even more, all of the formant frequencies exist simultaneously during speech with a continuous movement up and down the frequency spectrum depending on the spoken word. So what you hear when you listen to a person speaking is not a single frequency or waveform, but a number of overtones which have been filtered from glottal pulses.

An illustration of the frequency spectrum which results from the spoken word is shown in Fig. 2-8. Each of the acoustic

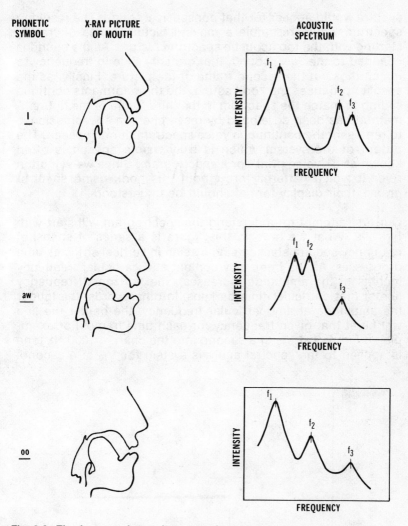

Fig. 2-8. The formant shapes in a speech spectrum.

spectra has a different formant frequency content because, in each of the three cases given, a different vowel sound is spoken. The peaks of the spectra, f_1, f_2 and f_3, represent the vocal tract resonances or formants which exist during normal speech.

Now using the preceding figure as a guide, imagine a person speaking the sounds "i-aw-oo" and how the time varying spectra would appear for that nonsensical sound. The resulting spectrum would resemble a moving picture series of frames starting with the top acoustic spectrum picture. As the sound is changed to the "aw" sound, the formants slide in frequency to match those in the second frame of the picture. Finally, as the speaker produces the "oo" sound, the three formants continue sliding to match the spectrum in the third frame of the figure. A method has been developed by researchers in speech science to represent the continuous voice spectrum during speech. The output of the system which is truly *visible* speech is often known as a "voice print" or a *spectrogram.* Since we will often refer to voice patterns throughout this book using spectrograms, their display format should be understood.

Our first attempt to understand the spectrogram will start with Fig. 2-9. What we have in this figure is a series of snapshot frequency spectra stacked side by side in vertical strips as time progresses. As the frequency content at a particular frequency increases (the amplitude increases), the horizontal frequency line at that particular time darkens. In other words, the louder the amplitude at any particular frequency, the darker the line will be at that given frequency for each time frame. For example, in Fig. 2-9 at $1/10$ of a second into the chart, a 1000 Hz tone is applied to the spectral analysis system for $1/10$ of a second.

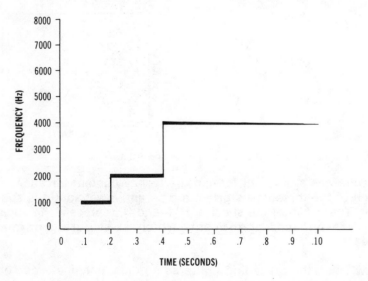

Fig. 2-9. A single tone spectrogram.

The tone is then increased to 2000 Hz for $^2/_{10}$ of a second at the same amplitude, then increased again to 4000 Hz at the same amplitude *but* allowed to decay in amplitude for the remainder of the one second period. Even though this is a rather simplified version of a spectrogram, it illustrates how the output can track the input frequency both in amplitude and frequency, giving a two-dimensional representation of the input versus time. Of course, if we were to inject two or more frequencies into the same type of analysis, then two or more darkened lines would appear and track the frequencies and amplitudes of the tones throughout the recording time. This is exactly the mechanism that occurs for recorded visible speech or spectrograms that will be referenced throughout the remainder of this book.

The "voice print" of the sound "ah" as in "father" is shown in Fig. 2-10 to familiarize you with the appearance of a typical spectrogram. Note that each of the darkened bars is a formant

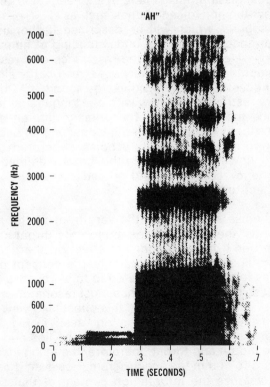

Fig. 2-10. Spectrogram of the sound "ah" (as in father).

frequency that exists throughout the spoken word. Now suppose you were to construct three voltage controlled bandpass filters and program their response to correspond in time with the movement of the dark bands given in the spectrogram. If the filters were fed simultaneously with a low frequency pulse resembling the glottal pulse, then the output of the time-varying filter system would very closely resemble the spoken sound in the spectrogram.

You have just been introduced to the design of a simple speech synthesizer based on formant synthesis used in many phonetic synthesis systems. We will look much closer at this technique in the chapter on synthesis methods.

THE RESONATED HISS

The final speech sound which we will attack in this chapter is the nonvocal hissing noise made by the teeth, lips, and tongue to represent the nonvoiced sounds such as *s, t, f, p, sh, ch,* and *k.* These sounds, which will be described further in the next chapter, are necessary to our understanding of human speech but are generated entirely by the resonance of a restricted air flow from our lungs. If, for instance, we restrict the air flow with our lips and teeth, then we produce the sound "f." On the other hand, if we restrict the air flow with our tongue and teeth, then we produce the sound "th." The primary difference between these two sounds is the amount of resonance that occurs to the almost uniform spectrum white noise generated by the restricted air flow. (White noise in this case is defined as a uniform frequency content sound spread across the audio frequency spectrum.)

Since the noise source is at the very front of the mouth for these sounds, the various resonators in the throat and rear of the mouth don't have a significant effect on the noise generated by the lips or teeth. Accordingly, the concept of formant frequencies for these sounds (referred to as fricative or plosive sounds) does not really apply since most resonators are "out of the circuit." An easier way to see this effect is to view the spectrogram of the fricative sound "s" in "seal" in Fig. 2-11. Very little filtering of the sound produced at the lips and teeth occurs in the mouth and throat; therefore, the resonances are extremely hard to find in the spectrogram. However, those that do exist characterize the information content of that sound and cause it to be heard as recognizable speech.

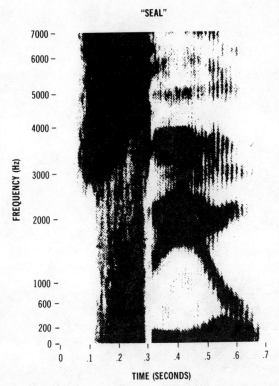

"SEAL"

Fig. 2-11. Spectrogram showing the "s" sound spectrum found in the word "seal."

In this chapter we've taken a look (although rather briefly) at the mechanism of human speech generation. The chapter began with rather biological concepts of the human speech system and ended with references to formant frequency synthetic speech techniques. We attempted to understand how the brain processes speech from the cognitive input to the final creation of sound. If you followed the chapter fairly closely, then you should have a cursory understanding of the mechanism by which humans create speech. This is the most basic foundation for the understanding of computer-generated synthetic speech.

Up until now we've ignored the language which is interpreted from the sounds generated by the vocal tract. As we move into the next chapter, we must, of course, assume that the English language is to be spoken as we analyze the next basic tool of speech science—linguistics.

chapter 3
A Word on Linguistics

It would be very convenient at this time to introduce you to the concepts and principles of synthetic speech generation. However, that is like saying "here's the computer; now write me a program to do income tax preparation." Although that statement sounds relatively direct and unambiguous, we have not specified the language in which the program will be written. We would be lost if we tried to understand the composition and generation of such a program without knowing the computer language to be used. If we attempted to examine and analyze the various speech synthesis methods without first taking a look at the fundamentals of the language to be spoken, we would be handicapped in the same manner. Although you might understand the complexities of speech synthesis without knowing some basics of linguistics, the information would do you very little good when the application of the synthesizer was considered. For this reason, we will examine briefly some of the more basic concepts of linguistics known as phonology and phonetics.

First of all, let's define the term linguistics. Linguistics is a noun meaning the science of language. If you had the next four or five years to read this chapter, then we might do this subject justice. Instead, we will briefly touch on the few areas of linguistics particularly appropriate to the understanding of synthetic speech technology and leave the remainder of the reading for those with a personal interest in language studies.

As you progress into this chapter, you should notice that its major emphasis is placed on the area of phonetic speech analysis. A word of explanation is needed for those of you who may question the need for a knowledge of phonemes when you're not really interested in phoneme (fō-,nēm) speech synthesizers. Let me cite an example to help solve this dilemma. Suppose at some time in the future you buy or have your speech synthesizer made and have it talking. *But,* it doesn't sound quite right when it says certain words. If you try to get advice or assistance from anyone having a knowledge of the English language and its makeup, he will probably tell you that certain phonemes are not being spoken correctly. If you don't have at least a basic understanding of this terminology, then you're not ready for his answer. Although you may not be a linguist after you finish this chapter, you should be able to talk intelligently with one and describe your synthesizer's speech output in technical terms. So, phonemes are basic to speech. Let's take a look at them.

Say Aaahhh

Everyone remembers going to the doctor as a youngster and having the tongue depressor placed in your mouth while hearing those infamous words "say aaahhh." The purpose of that exercise was to enable the doctor to see deeply into your throat. As you were pronouncing that sound, you were speaking one of the most basic elements of linguistics: a *phoneme.* The reason that particular phoneme was chosen as a universal test case for looking into people's throats is that it causes the resonators of the throat and mouth to relax, thereby giving the widest viewing angle. As we learned in the last chapter, the enlargement of these resonating cavities also produces a lowering of the primary resonant or formant frequencies.

As we begin to talk about the phonetic makeup of our typical English speech as heard in the United States, we must find some standard on which to base our sounds. The specific sounds to be discussed in this chapter will be taken from the General American (GA) dialect and the phonemes correspond to those from the alphabet of the International Phonetic Association (IPA). This alphabet cannot only be used to represent the speech sounds of the GA dialect, but can also represent most of the sounds from other languages throughout the world. In an attempt to avoid the confusing symbols used by the IPA (often found in the front of dictionaries), we will also describe phonemes and other speech sounds in terms of their pronunciation within English words.

One possible way of viewing the basic speech sounds and their relation to our final spoken intelligible language is to form a correlation between spoken language and computer language. (There is a great similarity. Of course, in one case you are conversing with humans, the other computers.) Consider, for instance, the case of the most basic computer instruction, machine code. If we can relate this to the basic speech sound, then we know we can take a number of sounds or phonemes in the proper order and create words. In a similar manner we can take a logical sequence of machine codes and create computer subroutines. Of course, these subroutines can be a part of a larger computer language, depending on their structure, such as BASIC, PASCAL, FORTRAN, etc. Similarly, the corresponding speech sounds or phonemes can be organized into many languages such as English, German, Spanish, etc. So we might look at a speech sound as equivalent to the most elementary machine code instruction while the spoken word would correspond to a higher level computer language program "line." If you were to then place a structured group of program lines together to form a complete program, you might have created a computer "sentence." So the analogy does exist between computer languages and spoken languages. An understanding of the basic elements of each helps the user to be an expert in his field whether it be computer language or spoken language.

In addition to phonemes within the structured English language, there are also other elements of speech which help to define the spoken sounds we call words. These variations on a spoken phoneme (of which there are approximately 40) are called allophones ('al-ə-,fōn). If we dissected the same phoneme used in 30 different words, we would probably have 30 variations in the way that particular phoneme is spoken. Each of these variations is known as an allophone. So, in effect, allophones are a much larger set of the basic 40 phonemes with an editorial license on the pronunciation of each sound. The variations present in the allophones depend not only on the particular phoneme and word being spoken but also on the position of the phoneme within the word.

Another element of speech which occurs during normal articulation is the diphthong ('dif,thon). Although the diphthong cannot be represented by a single symbol, it does have a characteristic sound which depends on a vocal tract motion from one phoneme to another. It typically stems from the pronunciation of two vowel-type phonemes in succession such as "ah" and "ee" (creating the sound i). It is, therefore, characterized by the change in sound between phonemes. Consequently, a diphthong cannot exist without being placed between two phonemes in a spoken sound.

If there are two allophonic variations of phonemes with an intervening diphthong, then the diphthong, of course, takes on a different sound. So it becomes obvious within the spoken English language that there are a large variety of sounds which are required to create *normal* sounding human speech. Chart 3-1 gives a representation of the International Phonetic Alphabet used in many pronunciation dictionaries. Not only must we consider all these sounds when describing a spoken word, but we must also consider the various diphthongs and allophones which coexist.

Although this discussion of the various phonetic and allphonic sounds can be rather discouraging to a computer enthusiast trying to reconstruct speech with electronic hardware, there is a light at the end of the tunnel. Perfectly recognizable speech can be constructed with a limited group of the possible combinations of phonemes, allophones, and diphthongs. Even though these sounds may differ slightly in pronunciation in the resultant speech, the difference in the meaning of the sounds will not be significant. Very often the computer spoken dialect resembles a foreign language accent and is largely understandable to most people.

The Vowel Sounds

The majority of the vowel sounds spoken in the General American (GA) speech are characterized by a relatively fixed position of the mouth and vocal tract with most of the sound emanating from the mouth opening. Very little if any nasal coupling occurs during the utterance of these sounds.

There are basically 12 vowels in the construction of the GA speech that relate to the English language. These are shown in Fig. 3-1.

Each of these vowels is shown with its approximate vocal tract profile to illustrate the position of the tongue within the mouth and its relation to the lips and teeth. Notice that, in particular, when the tongue is humped in the rear of the open mouth, the sounds that emanate approximate the "ah" sound as in the

Chart 3-1. The International Phonetic Alphabet (IPA).

Consonants

	Bilabial	Labio-dental	Dental and alveolar	Retroflex	Palato-alveolar	Alveolo-palatal	Palatal	Velar	Uvular	Pharyngal	Glottal
Plosive	p b		t d	ʈ ɖ			c ɟ	k g	q ɢ		ʔ
Nasal	m	ɱ	n	ɳ			ɲ	ŋ	ɴ		
Lateral Fricative			ɬ ɮ								
Lateral Nonfricative			l	ɭ			ʎ				
Rolled			r						ʀ		
Flapped			ɾ	ɽ					ʀ		
Fricative	ɸ β	f v	θ ð s z	ʂ ʐ	ʃ ʒ	ɕ ʑ	ç ʝ	x ɣ	χ ʁ	ħ ʕ	h ɦ
Frictionless Continuants and Semivowels	w ɥ	ʋ	ɹ				j (ɥ)	(w)	ʁ		

Vowels

	Front	Central	Back
Close	i y	ɨ u	ɯ u
Half-close	e ø	ə	o ɤ
Half-open	ɛ œ	ɜ	ɔ ʌ
Open	æ	a a	ɑ ɒ

Rounded: (y ʉ u), (ø o), (œ ɔ), (ɒ)

*Secondary articulations are shown by symbols in parentheses.

OTHER SOUNDS.—Palatalized consonants: ʈ, ɖ, etc. Velarized or pharyngalized consonants: ɫ, d̶, z̶, etc. Ejective consonants (plosives with simultaneous glottal stop): p', t', etc. Implosive voiced consonants: ɓ, ɗ, etc. ɼ fricative trill. σ, ʚ (labialized θ, ð, or s, z). ɋ, ʒ (labialized ʃ, ʒ). ʇ, ʗ, ʖ (clicks, Zulu c, q, x). ʟ (a sound between r and l). ʍ (voiceless w). ɪ, ʏ, ʊ (lowered varieties of i, y, u). ǝ (a variety of ǝ). ɵ (a vowel between ø and o).

Affricates are normally represented by groups of two consonants (ts, tʃ, dʒ, etc.), but, when necessary, ligatures are used (ʦ, ʧ, ʤ, etc.), or the marks ‿ or ͡ (t͡s or t͡ʃ, etc.). c, ɟ may occasionally be used in place of tʃ, dʒ. Aspirated plosives: ph, th, etc.

LENGTH, STRESS, PITCH.—ː (full length). ˑ (half length). ˈ (stress, placed at beginning of the stressed syllable). ˌ (secondary stress). ¯ (high level pitch); ˍ (low level); ´ (high rising); ˏ (low rising); ` (high falling); ˎ (low falling); ˆ (rise-fall); ˇ (fall-rise).

MODIFIERS.— ˜ nasality. ̥ breath (l̥ = breathed l). ̬ voice (s̬ = z). ʻslight aspiration following p, t, etc. ˔ specially close vowel (e̝ = a very close e). ˕ specially open vowel (e̞ = a rather open e). ̜ labialization (n̜ = labialized n). ̪ dental articulation (t̪ = dental t). ˒ palatalization (ź = ʒ). ˔ tongue slightly raised. ˕ tongue slightly lowered. ˒ lips more rounded. ˓ lips more spread. Central vowels i (= ɨ), ü (= ʉ), ë (= ɘ), ö (= ɵ), ɛ̈, ɔ̈; (e.g. n̩) syllabic consonant. ˘ consonantal vowel. ʃ variety of ʃ resembling s, etc.

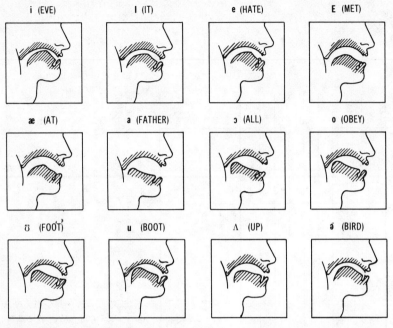

Fig. 3-1. The vowel phonemes and their vocal tract positions.

word "father." If you will open your mouth, say the word "ah," and hold your jaw in a fixed position with your hand, we will try a simple experiment. Without changing anything but the position of the tongue in your mouth while you are saying the phoneme "ah," slowly move your tongue toward the front of your mouth so it touches your lower teeth and notice how the sound changes to the "ee" sound as in the word "eve." Most of the vowel sounds are created by the position and shape of the tongue within a relatively fixed opening vocal tract. If you perform the last vowel experiment with your lips puckered as in a whistle, you should notice that the sound will change from the "ah" sound to the "oo" sound as in the word boot. If you would like to experiment further with the mouth configuration during vowel speech, try to approximate the positions of the tongue and lips in Fig. 3-1 and see how the vowel phonemes resemble those given.

The Other Sounds: Consonants

The consonant sounds (phonemes) make up the remainder of the spoken sounds within the English language. While the vowels described in the previous section require a relatively fixed mouth position during pronunciation, consonants are characterized by a more dynamic or moving set of mouth positions. There are a few consonants which do not require vocal tract motion during the pronunciation. These are described as continuants. The continuant consonants are most closely akin to the vowel sounds; however, they are typically much more complex in their spectral content because more of the vocal tract filtering mechanisms are brought into use.

There are basically five types of consonants which can be separately characterized as being used in English speech. These are:

1. Stop consonants.
2. Fricative consonants.
3. Nasal consonants.
4. Glide consonants.
5. Semi-vowel consonants.

The first of these, the *stop* consonants, are characterized by a rather active vocal tract movement in conjunction with a complete pause in speech output during the spoken phoneme. Although the pause may be as short as a tiny fraction of a second, without it the speech would not be normal.

There are six basic stop consonants which can be described in our language. Three of these are voiced with an accompanying oscillation of the vocal cords; three are voiceless requiring no glottal pulses during their release. The voiced stop consonants are:

B	as in butter
D	as in dog
G	as in green

As you pronounce the words which contain each of these voiced stop consonants very slowly, you should notice that there is a very short pause in your speech followed by a rather sudden release of air from your lungs which characterizes the stop. The three voiceless consonants have the same feature, but do not require a simultaneous oscillation of the vocal cords during their pronunciation. These three voiceless stop consonants are illustrated as follows:

P	as in paper
T	as in tomato
K	as in kick

Each of these voiceless stop consonants, as in the previous voiced ones, has a complete stop of speech during the pronunciation, but is not accompanied by the vocal cord vibrations. These are very similar in sound to the fricative consonants which follow.

The most characteristic feature of a *fricative* phoneme is the absence of specific formant frequencies. As we look at the nine identifiable fricatives you will see the reason. As in the previous stop consonants, there are voiced and unvoiced fricatives. The voiced fricatives, of which there are four, require both the glottal oscillation and the resonated hiss for pronunciation:

V	as in valve
TH	as in there
Z	as in zebra
ZH	as in azure

The remaining five unvoiced fricative consonants also contain the resonated hiss but do not require the simultaneous vocal cord vibration:

F	as in fanfare
TH	as in think
S	as in sound
SH	as in sugar
H	as in help

Each of the above fricative consonants has within it the use of the resonanted hiss to produce some of the highest frequency sounds of speech. Since they are all continuant phonemes, they require no vocal tract motion during their pronunciation.

The third type of consonant is referred to as a *nasal* consonant phoneme because the sound is primarily radiated through the nose. If you have a cold or the flu with the associated clogged nasal passage, then these sounds, as you recall, are the most difficult to pronounce correctly. In fact, if you will pinch your nose with your fingers and try to pronounce these sounds, the results of your speech will show you that these are strongly dependent upon the nasal cavity filtering. So, take a deep breath, hold your nose, and try these nasal consonants:

M	as in mike
N	as in noon
NG	as in ring

If you held your nose during the pronunciation of those three nasal phonemes, then you know where they get their name. The sounds that were actually spoken by you closely resemble bike, dude, and reek. In other words, the effect of the nasal filtering and coupling on the voiced speech output is absolutely required to produce the nasal phoneme sounds.

The last two consonant phonemes, *glides* and *semi-vowels,* are a very small group of the total English sounds. These most closely resemble the vowel sounds and are described by voiced excitation with very little nasal coupling. The *glides,* as their name implies, are dynamic, requiring motion of the mouth to complete their pronunciation:

Y	as in yoyo
W	as in winter

Since these phonemes are dynamic and require a motion of the mouth to produce, they are not continuants. The *semi-vowels* being vowel-like in nature are continuants and can be produced for prolonged periods of time. There are only two semi-vowels which are identifiable as definite phonemes:

R	as in run
L	as in list

That completes the list of definitive English phonemes required to produce recognizable speech and characterize the spoken English language. Variations in the previously described phonemes do exist and are referred to as *diphthongs* produced by saying two vowel phonemes in succession. Affricates are similarly produced between the pronunciation of two successive consonants.

Onward and Upward

Our observations in this chapter so far have dealt with the smallest basic sound of the English spoken language, the phoneme. Obviously, speech is not completely describable in terms of phonemes because of the physical variations and emotions of the speaker. The sound of each phoneme spoken (as described earlier) is also highly dependent upon the group of phonemes surrounding each sound. As we begin to string phonemes together to create more intelligible phrases, we have spoken words. The composition of a word can be analyzed linguistically in terms other than phonemes with *morphemes, morphs,* and *allomorphs.* These units of speech are rather complex in their definition and depend not only on sounds within the word but also the meanings of the word. Since the study of word meanings and associated grammar is beyond our current interest in creating synthetic speech, we will just assume that they exist within the spoken words. Further reading in the area of word segmentation can be found in the suggested readings at the end of this book.

As phonemes are strung together to create the longer intelligible sounds known as words, there are a number of quantitative features we can extract from them. Although, as mentioned earlier, the true pronunciation of each phoneme is strongly dependent upon its placement within a word, certain sound features of each hold constant throughout average human speech. This information can also be used to plan and compare computer-generated speech with "ideal" human speech.

Take, for example, the frequency of occurrence of common words within the spoken English language. Given this list of words, a speech synthesizer should, at the very least, pronounce each of these accurately because they are the ones which will be spoken most often. Such a list of words compiled many years ago by Godfrey Duey at Harvard University is shown in Table 3-1. The words are listed in descending order. The most frequently spoken word is given at the top with the relative frequency of occurrence beside each word. The proper way to interpret this table would be, for instance, to say that the word "the" occurs slightly more than 7 times out of 100 words. The next most frequent word "of" occurs almost 4 times out of 100 words and so on. This table can be used in several ways. As an exercise, your speech synthesizer should be made to practice each of these words and to confirm that they are correctly pronounced, because these will be the most frequently spoken words. An alternative use for this table (if you have a stored vocabulary in your speech synthesizer system) will be to tell you which words as a minimum to store in your vocabulary.

If the same principle is taken one step further, then we can also analyze the most frequently spoken speech sounds (Table 3-2).

Table 3-1. The Most Frequently Spoken Words

Rank	Word	Percentage of Occurrence	Rank	Word	Percentage of Occurrence
1	the	7.31	51	when	.23
2	of	3.99	52	him	.23
3	and	3.28	53	them	.22
4	to	2.92	54	her	.22
5	a	2.12	55	am	.21
6	in	2.11	56	your	.21
7	that	1.34	57	any	.21
8	it	1.21	58	more	.21
9	is	1.21	59	now	.21
10	I	1.15	60	its	.20
11	for	1.03	61	time	.20
12	be	.84	62	up	.20
13	was	.83	63	do	.20
14	as	.78	64	out	.20
15	you	.77	65	can	.19
16	with	.72	66	than	.19
17	he	.68	67	only	.18
18	on	.64	68	she	.18
19	have	.61	69	made	.17
20	by	.60	70	other	.16
21	not	.58	71	into	.16
22	at	.58	72	men	.16
23	this	.57	73	must	.16
24	are	.54	74	people	.16
25	we	.52	75	said	.16
26	his	.51	76	may	.16
27	but	.50	77	man	.15
28	they	.47	78	about	.15
29	all	.46	79	over	.15
30	or	.45	80	some	.15
31	which	.45	81	these	.15
32	will	.44	82	two	.14
33	from	.43	83	very	.14
34	had	.41	84	before	.13
35	has	.39	85	great	.13
36	one	.36	86	could	.13
37	our	.33	87	such	.13
38	an	.33	88	first	.13
39	been	.32	89	upon	.12
40	no	.32	90	every	.12
41	their	.31	91	how	.12
42	there	.30	92	come	.12
43	were	.30	93	us	.12
44	so	.30	94	shall	.12
45	my	.29	95	should	.11
46	if	.26	96	then	.11
47	me	.25	97	like	.11
48	what	.25	98	will	.11
49	would	.25	99	little	.11
50	who	.24	100	say	.11

Table 3-2. Frequency of Occurrence for Speech Sounds

Rank	Sound	"as in"	Percentage of Occurrence
1	i	tip	7.94
2	n	navy	7.24
3	t	tot	7.13
4	r	rare	6.88
5	uh	ton	5.02
6	s	sis	4.55
7	d	dad	4.31
8	ae	tap	4.17
9	ee	feet	3.89
10	1	lilly	3.74
11	eh	ten	3.44
12	th	then	3.43
13	ah	top	3.33
14	z	zebra	2.97
15	m	mama	2.78
16	k	kick	2.71
17	a	tape	2.35
18	v	vivacious	2.28
19	w	wine	2.08
20	p	paper	2.04
21	f	fluffy	1.84
22	h	hat	1.81
23	b	bob	1.81
24	oh	tone	1.63
25	oo	tool	1.60
26	I	bike	1.59
27	aw	talk	1.26
28	ng	sing	0.96
29	sh	sugar	0.82
30	g	go	0.74
31	u	took	0.69
32	y	yoyo	0.60
33	ou	our	0.59 (dipthong)
34	ch	chalk	0.52
35	j	judge	0.44
36	th	thick	0.37
37	ew	few	0.31 (dipthong)
38	oi	boil	0.09 (dipthong)
39	zh	azure	0.05

This will apply not only to phonetic synthesis systems but also will ensure correct pronunciation of the sounds in any speech synthesis system. Each of the sounds (or phonemes) is given with its relative frequency of occurrence and an associated word use of that sound. This table can be used to illustrate the most commonly used phonemes. It can also show you which sounds or phonemes may be omitted in a more simplistic system. That is to say that if you were interested in constructing an elementary phonetic speech synthesizer system, then those sounds or phonemes with very low usage rates such as "zh" as in "azure" and the diphthong "oi" as in "oil" could possibly be omitted. Such phonemes as "i" as in "tip" with a relatively high occurrence must be included because they are the most used phonemes. There is more information about phonemes that may help you in constructing and analyzing your speech synthesizer. This is the relative phonetic power that exists between each spoken phoneme by the average speaker. Such a table of relative powers is given in Table 3-3.

From this table, we can investigate each of the most used phonemes in terms of their relative power or loudness so that we can ensure that our computer speech resembles the characteristics of human speech. Table 3-3 lists each phoneme with an associated example word and the loudness of that phoneme

Table 3-3. Relative Power of Speech Sounds

Rank	Sound	"as in"	Relative Power
1	aw	talk	680
2	ah	top	600
3	uh	ton	510
4	ae	tap	490
5	oh	tone	470
6	u̲	took	460
7	a̅	tape	370
8	eh̲	ten	350
9	oo	tool	310
10	i̲	tip	260
11	ee	peek	220
12	r	rare	210
13	l	lilly	100
14	sh	sugar	80
15	ng	sing	73
16	m	mama	52
17	ch	church	42
18	n	Nancy	36
19	j	judge	23
20	zh	azure	20
21	z	zoo	16
22	s	sis	16
23	t	tot	15
24	g	go	15
25	k	cook	13
26	v	vote	12
27	th̲	that	11
28	b̲	bob	7
29	d	dad	7
30	p	paper	6
31	f	fluffy	5
32	th	thick	1

in relation to the others in the table. The most powerful of the phonemes, "aw" as in "talk," is 680 times greater than the phoneme "th" as in "thin." This level can also be expressed in decibels (dB) with a difference of 28 dB. Notice that all of the vowel sounds are the most prominent in terms of loudness with the glides and nasals following. Finally filling out the remainder of the list are the fricative consonant phonemes which are spoken most softly. Of course, these values given in this table do not take into account the use of accents on syllables which may increase or decrease certain phoneme loudness relationships. The values given here are for an average group of phonemes spoken during normal conversation.

The three previous tables can be used to exercise and evaluate any synthetic speech system. Of course, the ultimate results of any testing depend on the listening ear. No matter how technically correct the speech is in terms of human speech, the final result and judgment on the quality of the computer speech will be given by the human listener. The use of these tables will, however, help to ensure that your synthetic speech system approximates the quantitative features of normal human conversation. If you would really like to evaluate your synthetic speech system in terms of its linguistic capabilities, then you should prepare a series of test words to exercise each of the phoneme sounds used within normal speech. In an ideal case, a test can be performed with a friend or relative who has never heard your speech system. A list of vocabulary words is spoken by your computer for them so that you may evaluate the percentage of understanding of each individual word. The words or group of words that are *not* correctly understood by the unbiased listener indicates a weakness in that particular phoneme or group of phonemes from your synthesizer. If you would like to try that experiment and you have the capability for programming full speech vocabulary from your synthesizer, then the next section of this chapter will help you to evaluate your system.

This Is a Test

At some point in your experimentation and interest with speech synthesizers, you will finally have created a machine that talks. You may, if you desire, simply be satisfied with the talking capability if you alone intend to listen to it. However, if you intend for others who are not "trained listeners" to understand your system, then you should ensure that it has the capability for correct universal pronunciation. In the following pages are a list of words which serve as an articulation drill for your speech synthesizer. These words may be programmed into your memory by the means available to your system and then spoken either in sequence or at random to verify the correct pronunciation. If an untrained listener can correctly identify each of the words from the list, then your system has a very accurate pronunciation. The words which are misunderstood indicate a weakness in that particular phonetic area, and either the programming or volume level of that particular sound should be altered. A set of words for each phoneme is given. See if you can identify each phoneme used within the word groups. The answers will be given following the articulation drill.

1. Saw, Horse, Horn, Ball, Talk
2. Yard, Clock, Top, Block, Star, Arm
3. Gloves, Rug, Truck, Tub, Button, Ton
4. Tap, Hat, Can, Black, Grass, Basket
5. Tone, Boat, Coat, Snow, Stove, Comb
6. Book, Cook, Foot, Look, Took
7. Tape, Cake, Grapes, Table, Lady, Tail
8. Ten, Bed, Dress, Red, Steps, Feather, Sled
9. Tool, Blue, Moon, Tooth, Shoe
10. Tip, Chicken, Fish, Pillow, Pig
11. Peek, Cheese, Meat, Sleep, Trees, Green, Feet
12. Radio, Rake, Barrel, Car, Tire, Rabbit, Red
13. Ladder, Lease, Leg, Letter, Ball, Bottle, Look
14. Sheep, Shelf, Dish, Fish, Brush, Push, Shoulder, Shake
15. Finger, Sing, Swinging, Ring, Tongue, Blanket
16. Move, Music, Memory, Most, More, Meek, Mimic, Movie
17. Chair, Cheese, Chicken, Watch, Catch, Matches, Teacher, Speech, Church
18. Nasal, Know, Knife, Candle, Woman, Nancy, Spoon, Man
19. Juice, Engine, Orange, Soldier, Bridge, Joke, Jump
20. Glacier, Azure, Measure, Television
21. Music, Zoo, Roses, Ears, Nose, Zebra, Scissors
22. Seven, See, Saw, Sleep, Spoon, Basket, Glasses, Face
23. Table, Tire, Butter, Tot, Letter, White
24. Gloves, Grass, Gun, Golf, Digging, Wagon, Rug, Flag
25. Crack, Pocket, Black, Clock, Cook, Fake
26. Vase, Violet, Vivacious, Cover, Drive, River, Stove
27. Thimble, Three, Thin, Thick, Mouth, Teeth
28. Bed, Boat, Rabbit, Ribbon, Umbrella, Table, Bob
29. Dog, Drink, Indian, Radio, Dud, Bed, Wood
30. Paper, Pencil, Airplane, Apple, Pop, Cap, Rope, Sleep

31. Feather, Finger, Fire, Fluffy, Elephant, Laugh, Roof, Knife
32. These, Those, Brother, Then, Father, Feather, Loathe

Each of the 32 major phonemes given in the previous list is required for adequate speech understanding from a speech synthesizer. If the synthesizer under test has a problem with any of the numbered groups of words, then its deficiencies can be pinpointed to specific phonemes by determining which group of words the mispronounced or misunderstood sound is in. As you read through the list, you should have been able to identify each of the specific phonemes from the previous reading in this chapter. If you had trouble identifying some of the groups, then don't worry, the answers are given here.

Item	Phoneme	Word
1.	aw	talk
2.	ah	top
3.	uh	ton
4.	ae	tap
5.	oh	tone
6.	u	took
7.	a	tape
8.	eh	ten
9.	oo	tool
10.	i	tip
11.	ee	peek
12.	r	rake
13.	l	look
14.	sh	shake
15.	ng	ring
16.	m	move
17.	ch	church
18.	n	Nancy
19.	j	joke
20.	zh	azure
21.	z	zoo
22.	s	see
23.	t	tot
24.	g	golf
25.	k	cook
26.	v	vivacious
27.	*th*	thick
28.	b	bob
29.	d	dud

30.	p	pop
31.	f	fluffy
32.	th	then

The previous test is appropriate for any speech synthesizer or, for that matter, any speaking person to test and exercise the correct pronunciation of the various classes of phonemes. As you become more knowledgeable in the field of synthetic speech, then a test such as this is an appropriate means of determining the capabilities of *any* speech synthesizer. It may also be used to compare qualities of speech for comparative purposes.

A Final Word on Linguistics

The field of linguistics and the technology of synthetic speech are intertwined at a very deep level. If you have no intention of programming sounds or generating connected speech from phonemes, then the previous phonetic information may help you only to investigate other synthetic speech capabilities. If you, on the other hand, are creating original speech from speech sounds with a phonetic speech synthesizer, then you should perform a phonetic inventory of your system. This will ensure that the sounds are pronounced as you intend them to be. Remember, though, that another person or unbiased observer may perceive the sounds in a completely different manner than you.

Another important consideration when creating speech for listeners other than yourself is to realize that within North American English speech there are a very large number of dialects in existence. A dialect, a regional variety of a language, differs distinctly from the standard language in the use of certain grammatical forms and pronunciations. As you begin to program your computer with speech, you will unconsciously program in your own dialect. If you were to let another person across the country hear your vocal programming, he might be able to identify the area from which it came.

The best way to avoid programming your own dialect into a system is to carefully listen to national television programming. Network programs such as news broadcasts and other shows should give you a goal for the speech sounds from your computer. Only then will your system have that "broadcast quality-type speech" that is most easily understood by people across the country.

Another brief item for your linguistic consideration: in programming computer phrases from your computer, you should take grammatical forms into account depending on the area of the country in which your speech system will be used. For instance, did you realize that depending on where you live, the center of a cherry may be referred to as a pit, a seed, or a stone. Each of these words has the same meaning in its own location, but it may have a completely different meaning when taken to another part of the country. Another example of such regional speech differences is the location description kitty-corner and catty-corner. A person from the north or south would most likely understand both phrases; however, they sound rather strange when used in opposite parts of the country. In reviewing this somewhat specialized field of linguistics, I am not saying that your computer speech must be grammatically perfect. I am, instead, trying to make you aware that speech differences occur throughout a language's spoken territory. To be equally well received in all areas, the speech should be the most neutral that can be obtained. That speech is found most often in network television broadcasts.

In summary, a thorough understanding and use of the elements of linguistics will provide you and your synthetic speech system with a well-rounded and well-understood vocabulary. The more time and consideration you put in the study of linguistics as you begin to teach your computer to talk, the more intelligent and articulate it will appear. Of course, grammar and sentence construction cannot be neglected, but that study is "old hat" for all of us. If you have questions concerning sentence structure to be spoken, then refer to the readings at the end of the book. Just remember to be careful with sentence construction. The meaning of a phrase that you intend for your computer to say may be interpreted in a completely different manner by another person. I give in closing the evidence to ponder:

> Time flies like an arrow.
> Fruit flies like a banana.

chapter 4

Computer Speech Etiquette

The two preceding chapters have dealt with the generation of human speech ranging from the most basic sounds to the formation of English words. You should now have a relatively firm foundation for proceeding into the realm of computer-generated speech. However, at some point between the two apparently identical concepts of human and computer speech, there is a rather gray field. This gap is bridged by intelligence. And the intelligence I am speaking of is not that of the readers, but rather that of the speakers. In this chapter, we will take a rather light-hearted look at the fundamental intelligence behind a spoken phrase and how the circumstances may differ between human and nonhuman speakers.

Although the information in this chapter may be considered rather off-the-wall by the computer speech purists, the information presented here is extremely important to the practical application of computer-generated speech. Its consideration in a final product application can determine the success or failure of a real world system. The type of information to be discussed deals with interfacing computer-generated speech to the human ear.

When you speak a phrase, you take many outside influencing factors into consideration to determine how or when that phrase is spoken. The computer on the other hand, unless it is extremely well "trained" or has artificial intelligence, does not. The purpose of this chapter will be to make you aware of these differences. You will learn to allow for some preplanning in the timeliness and consideration of your computer as it begins to speak.

Cater's Laws of Computer Speech

As an introduction to computer speech etiquette, let's look at some basic rules by which your computer should be speaking. As we proceed through the chapter, we will examine these laws and corollaries in more detail and try to relate their meaning to the application of computer synthetic speech. I suggest at this point that you go get yourself a cup of coffee, sit back in your easy chair with this book, and get ready to ponder overwhelmingly important thoughts for the next five minutes. Ready? Then here we go:

1. If a computer can say something at the wrong time, it will.
2. If you repeatedly demonstrate your talking computer to the same people, then they will expect an improvement in the quality of speech each time they hear the system talk.
3. People can be *told* to be quiet if you get tired of hearing them talk. A preprogrammed computer generating synthetic speech cannot.
4. Computers, like people, interrupting a conversation are rude. Ideally, a computer should be keyed to speak during room silence.
5. A short, unexpected computer spoken phrase will be lost in the clamor of normal conversation.
6. An important computer spoken announcement should be preceded by an annunciator tone or attention-getting sound.
7. A talking computer is like a child; it knows how to talk but not when to talk.
8. A computer that talks too much will be turned off.
9. A computer that talks too little will be ignored.
10. The listener should be preconditioned to expect a synthetic voice from your computer if the words are not spoken in a natural voice.

These laws are of profound importance as you begin to bring your talking computer out of the closet. Of course, the first words of speech may come with understandable exhilaration, but try to realize that the novelty of computer speech *will* wear off. At that instant you must begin applying the previous laws of computer speech etiquette to your operating system. By doing this you add a form of artificial intelligence to your speech operating system to make it a pleasant thing to be around. Otherwise, you might expect one day to find your computer's loudspeaker in the nearest trash can.

Obey the Law!

Even if you understand the general principles of the laws stated above, you might still be unsure of how to go about implementing them in your own talking computer system. That is where your own creativity can really make you sparkle. Most of the concepts introduced here are still relatively premature for the subject of computer-generated speech. The important thing to remember when applying these rules is that you are a biased observer. You nurtured your computer with loving care into its first few words of speech and at that point you are overcome with the novelty of a new capability. However, you must eventually put your own excitement aside and begin to train your talking machine for other ears. Other listeners, of course, will expect your system to be almost superhuman in its speech capabilities because it is a COMPUTER.

The most prevalent desire for those hearing a talking computer for the first time is to say "what did it say?" At that time you must swallow your pride and calmly repeat the spoken phrase in real speech so that they may understand the information supposedly transmitted by your computer. As you repeat the computer-generated phrase from your computer, the normal response is "yes, I think I can hear it."

A simple procedure that you may follow to alleviate the previous problem which normally occurs because the computer speaks as a person interrupts is to precede your computer-spoken message by either a tone, bell sound, or even a "clearing" of your computer's throat. This may, at first, seem like a silly gesture, but if you stop to consider in the course of normal human speech, no one begins speaking to you without first getting your attention in some manner. Normally this may be through a visible reaction or glance, or possibly a raising of the hand to inform you that their speech is coming. Why should your computer begin speaking without observing the same rules? What I am describing here is a virtual "hand shake" between humans before conversation can begin. Your computer should be expected to observe the same rules since it is supposed to have intelligence. There are other methods by which the computer-spoken announcement can be preannounced depending upon the interchange circumstances. For instance, if a person is sitting at a desk awaiting a computer-spoken phrase with his full attention on the computer, then an annunciator lamp can be illuminated prior to the spoken phrase to announce the output of a voice message. As mentioned earlier, a preceding tone or bell sound can also serve the same purpose. Do not, however, make the mistake of immediately following the annunciated message with the spoken phrase because if there is human conversation in progress, it will probably take two to three seconds to finish the sentence. So a good rule of thumb is to precede the spoken message with a warning followed by about two to three seconds of silence. If you plan to use your vocal output system in a large room or location where the computer is not immediately visible, then an audio tone or annunciator precursor should be utilized to signal the listener that a message is coming.

The application of the previous rule is of major importance in assuring a successful acceptance of your computer speech system. If you neglect the speech awaiting output annunciator, then most assuredly your message will be lost in the existing human conversation going on around the computer. Another method which may be used to accomplish this same purpose is to repeat the phrase several times. This, however, can become very trying on the listener unless the message is for emergency purposes. For instance, if the computer is signaling that there is a fire or security alert such as a break-in to a residence or business, then the message should not only be preceded by warning tones and attention-getting sounds, but should also be repeated at a very loud volume until the warning is acknowledged by the human operator. This brings up the next question. What means of interaction do we have with the computer during or after the spoken phrase? The answer to the question at this time is simple: none. For your next consideration we will introduce a few examples of feedback methods to your speech output system to give it some of that necessary human-like courtesy.

Now Can I Say It?

Our attempts in the previous section in interacting with the user might be considered totally passive in that the computer attempts to warn of upcoming speech output. To obtain true speech interaction capabilities with the operator, the system should respond to some form of input. In keeping with the concept of audio information exchange, this feedback should rightfully be through audible means. This does not mean that your computer has to understand spoken words or have the capability for speech recognition. Although the incorporation of this type of response system would be ideal and allow conversations to occur between you and your computer, it is not necessary in providing acoustic interaction. You will, however, still need a microphone input to your system to achieve a level of apparent computer intelligence.

The most simple audio input peripheral that you may attach to your computer is a microphone amplifier combination with a simple amplitude detector/threshold circuit to notify your computer of ongoing local audio activity. What this input device tells your computer is that there is currently local sound activity occurring and that the spoken phrase to the output should be "spooled" until the sound decays. (Spooling is temporary storage in memory of the output.) Fig. 4-1 shows the block diagram for a rather crude, but still effective, audio input system. The means by which the peripheral is used in software determines its apparent level of intelligence when interacting with the human listener. As shown in the diagram, the microphone should be placed in an area near the computer loudspeaker with the amplifier, detector, and threshold circuit set to a level so that the output logic level of the system is zero during normal ambient sound. If a person is speaking within listening distance of the computer output speaker, then the threshold should be set to provide a logic level 1 to the computer input

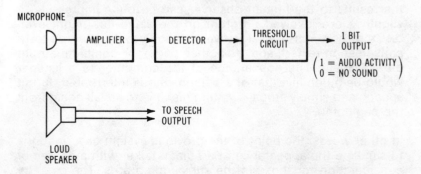

Fig. 4-1. Aural interaction diagram.

port. By testing this bit in software during an attempted speech output, the computer software can determine the best time to speak the phrase. The flow of a typical software system which will appear to add tremendous intelligence to your computer speech system is shown in Fig. 4-2.

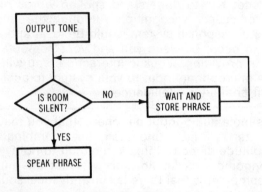

Fig. 4-2. Courteous computer speech flowchart.

The first step before beginning speech output is the annunciator tone or voiced interruption signal to alert the listener that sound is on its way. The computer should then pause momentarily for approximately one second to determine if the room has become silent by testing the output line from the audio interaction circuitry. If the conversation is continuing, then the phrase should be stored or "spooled" and the test for room silence repeated until the local noise level drops below threshold. At that time, the computer may then begin to speak its output phrase with relative assurance that there will not be conflicting audio within the room. The task of performing this noninterruption program is extremely simple in software, but the results to the human observer can be quite impressive. A slightly more involved program on the same line might even test the room noise level between specific output words for a conversation restart, and, if so, then begin the complete output phrase again. The appearance of the computer to a listener would be much like that of a person who is interrupted during speech and simply stops, awaiting his time to speak again from the beginning.

In other words, the point of the previous system description is to simulate the appearance of a human talker with a degree of consideration for those in the surrounding area. The circuitry for implementing the previous aural interaction scheme is

shown in Fig. 4-3. The circuit consists of three common integrated circuit type operational amplifiers used to provide amplification for a microphone, followed by the detection of the incoming audio and subsequent thresholding to overcome room noises. There are two adjustments provided in the circuitry; one for microphone gain, the other for ambient noise threshold adjustment. In practice, the audio interaction circuit would be interfaced to a single *input* port bit of your talking computer. This is the signal line which should be tested to determine if the room is silent or acoustically active. With the threshold adjustment set at approximately mid-point on its range, the gain adjustment should be set so that a person talking in a normal voice within the room will cause the input bit to the computer to be a logic 1 level or approximately 5 volts.

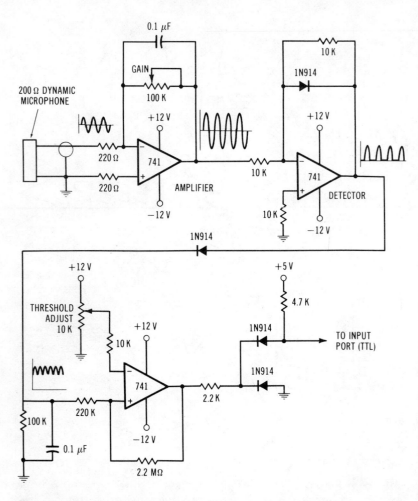

Fig. 4-3. A practical circuit for audio input.

Then when the person ceases talking, the level at the computer input port should quickly drop to a 0 volt input. All components within this circuitry are noncritical as is the wiring configuration. The only caution to be observed in constructing this circuitry is the shielding of the microphone line and connections to the input amplifier to assure that there is no hum or noise pickup. If you complete the circuit and attach it to your computer input port, through the parallel interface described, then with the extremely small amount of software required to implement the block diagram in Fig. 4-2, you have created a very intelligent-appearing talking computer.

Get Smarter

A more advanced audio input peripheral would, of course, be a speech recognition system which could not only acknowledge audio input but recognize your spoken words. The complexity of these devices and their variety of technologies could fill a book the size of this one. Rather than delve into these complex devices and how they could be implemented, let's assume that they exist and can be interfaced to an appropriate input port of your talking computer. Once you have accomplished this somewhat monumental task of intelligent audio input *and* output, you are limited only by your imagination in the things your computer can do with speech. For instance, if you have a speech recognition system that is capable of recognizing, say 16 words, then you have the capability for inputting yes, no, stop, what?, say again, louder, softer, etc. As you begin to work with the interaction software for speech output and intelligent input, you might find yourself soon throwing away the old keyboard. Realistically, though, you still have to input the words for which the system is not trained.

As you begin to enhance the speech programming or artificial intelligence of your computer system, you might create a speech training program which would allow you to input a word from the keyboard and have the computer attempt to speak the word correctly by trial and error in response to your verbal commands. Of course, this form of speech output and input interaction is limited primarily to the phonetic based systems to be described later. Other types could also be used if the stored speech vocabulary is large enough. The effects of verbal interaction with your computer as it begins to learn speech can be startling not only to yourself but to educated onlookers. The implementation of such an imaginative artificial intelligence speech system will be left up to your own creativity; however, computer capabilities of this complexity will surely exist within the next five to ten years. The hardware capabilities exist now; all that is lacking is the software to drive the system.

Minimal Considerations

Even if you decide not to create an aural input for your speaking computer system, you should still have a means of human interaction with your speech output. Remember, this output peripheral is not like a printer which can be left unattended for later perusal of the output. Speech output must be heard and understood in real time. In fact, a program that generates a considerable amount of speech output can often become very annoying without some method for either lowering the volume of the speech or completely shutting it off. If you have ever walked through an electronic game arcade and heard some of the babbling video games with their nonsensical voices, you should then understand the ultimate requirement for some operator control over the vocal output. If not, then go stand by one for 30 minutes and see if you don't agree.

The two controls suggested earlier are required as a minimum for a speech synthesizer to be considered well mannered. A volume control can be used by the operator to adjust the speech loudness as he desires. An on-off switch is also a requirement for the loudspeaker audio line. Alternatively a power switch on the speech synthesizer housing will serve the same purpose. This will allow any person listening to the speech out-

put to momentarily disable that output without having to change the volume level from a preset one. With these two controls at the operator's disposal, he has the capability of shutting off the synthesizer and controlling its output volume from a whisper to a shout.

Freedom of Speech?

As we begin to create talking machines that have the capability of getting our attention through audible suggestions, we are beginning to be subjected to a form of technology shock based on the absence of silence. A relatively good example of how technology is changing our surroundings is to observe the noise level in a quiet crowd, such as at church or in a theater, on the hour mark. You should notice an assortment of dings, clangs, beeps, and beep-beeps as the watches, calculators, and other electronic gadgets announce the passing of an hour mark. Imagine the results as the watches and calculators begin

to talk and announce the time. The confusion of all of the talking systems and various voices and accents will be certain. Furthermore, as the fixed machines such as typewriters, alarm clocks, ovens and stoves, refrigerators, and cars begin to talk, we will be continuously surrounded with strange voices from which we cannot retreat. Carefully consider the consequences of speech output in products or devices that you may come in contact with or design. Remember, computer speech output is a useful tool when not abused. Not every application requires a vocal response, and many will suffer from a lack of visual responses. Since you are now dealing with a computer response which cannot be ignored by simply looking away, you must be more responsible in choosing the form and content of the ultimate output message.

chapter 5

Speech Synthesis:
An Historical Review

Before we jump headlong into the technology of electronic speech synthesis, it may be of interest to you to briefly explore the early efforts of man to create that magical capability of speech which, for unknown reasons, was awarded only to the human. In the early Greek and Roman civilizations the people and the high priests took the ability of speech as a divine ordinance. This obsession with man's capability of speech was so revered that the pagan priests, in an effort to convince their followers of the authenticity of their idols and statues of gods, tried to make them speak to the people. Their technology at the time was, of course, very crude and their understanding of the speech mechanism even cruder; so these historical "con" men had to resort to the use of speaking tubes and cleverly concealed tunnels leading to the mouths of the statues. Imagine if today's technology could be applied to the unknowing people of those times. What their amazement would be at truly talking idols and false gods!

As time passed, there was a continual fascination with man's capability of speech. Various efforts, some quite feeble, were made to artificially create those sounds from machines. Some of the earlier documented attempts in this area came as civilization entered the Renaissance. Previously, research in the area of artificial speech generation had been based more in the qualitative understanding of the speech mechanism without much consideration for the underlying principles of speech. What the Renaissance did for man was to drive him into a scientific curiosity about life and physiological functions with no holds barred. One of the old challenges to be taken off the shelf was the study of human physiology and quantitative descriptions of the human speech mechanism. As the historical scientists began to study the physiology of speech, they began to formulate practical models of talking machines. Some were even constructed. Considering the state of science around the time the United States was being formed in the late 1700s, these talking machine models were really quite creative.

Talking Mechanisms

Before the age of electronics, scientists were hindered (in terms of our technology) in that they had no transistors or integrated circuits to fill their talking boxes. They, instead, had to rely on the science of mechanisms that they knew. Much like Charles Babbage's room-sized analytical machine "computer," constructed solely of mechanical parts, the early talking machines were more like musical instruments than the complex systems we might expect. The mechanical technology used at that time should not be taken lightly. Research efforts at constructing mechanical voice systems are still ongoing in parallel development with electronic synthesis methods.

One of the first attempts at mechanical speech generation, in recorded history, occurred around 1770 at the Imperial Academy of St. Petersburg (now Leningrad, USSR). In response to the university's challenge to explain the physiological speech differences between five vowels, Kratzenstein won the annual prize for modeling and constructing a series of acoustic resonators patterned after the human vocal tract. The speaking device, crude by today's standards, did, however, create the vowel sounds with vibrating reeds activated by air passage over them. By varying the acoustic resonators and effectively selecting the formant frequencies by hand, limited speech was generated by this mechanical device.

Unknown to Kratzenstein at the time, Wolfgang von Kempelen was working in parallel on a more elaborate speaking machine for generating connected speech. He had not been challenged with the replication of vowel sounds and, therefore, had aimed at a more complex target of creating phrases and multiple word sounds. As with Kratzenstein's device, his system employed a bellows to supply air for a vibrating reed which served as the vocal cords. The resonators of the mouth were simulated by a flexible cylindrical leather tube which, through hand manipulation, could produce voiced sounds. The strange mechanical device depicted in Fig. 5-1 also had openings to simulate the nasal resonators and two lever operated whistle tubes to create the fricative type sounds from the teeth and lips. The device was quite ingenious but required a considerable amount of skill and experience of the operator. As he "played" the device, he had to perform simultaneous actions not unlike those required to play the large musical organs of those times. Surprisingly enough, the talking machine had considerable human engineering built in so that a single operator could produce truly synthetic speech. As he sat beside the speaking machine with his right arm resting on the bellows, he controlled the nostril openings, the reed bypass plunger, and the whistle levers with his right hand. His left hand was free to manipulate the leather speech tube to articulate the voiced sounds from the vibrating reed. According to von Kempelen, his machine produced 19

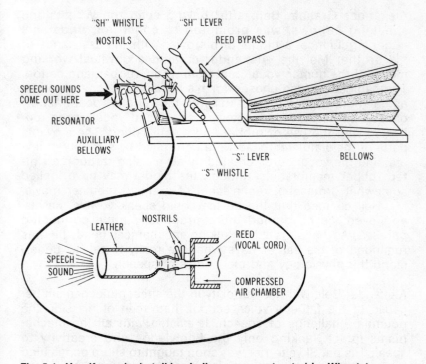

Fig. 5-1. Von Kempelen's talking bellows as constructed by Wheatstone.

73

consonant sounds which could be understood. Whether those sounds could be equally well understood by people other than von Kempelen might be questioned because of the operator bias mentioned in Chapter 4 of this book.

Although the previous "speaking bellows" conceived by von Kempelen was ultimately refined and constructed by Sir Charles Wheatstone (of the Wheatstone Bridge), very little research in similar directions followed until the turn of the 19th century. In the late 1800s, a young experimenter from Edinburgh, Scotland had a chance to view von Kempelen's machine as constructed by Wheatstone. The impression that this mechanical speaking device made on the young Alexander Graham Bell not only influenced the direction of his interest in the scientific field of speech, but also probably had a far reaching effect on the evolution of modern science. Some years later in February of 1876 he applied for and was granted U. S. Patent No. 174,465 describing the workings and practicality of a device called the telephone.

Alexander Graham Bell, after having seen the Wheatstone speaking bellows, was prompted to construct, under his father's guidance, a model of his own. With the assistance of his brother Melville, Alexander created a physical working model of the human vocal tract from wood, rubber, and cotton. The cabinet or case chosen for his speaking machine was an actual mold of the human skull with the various vocal tract organs such as the lips, cheeks, tongue, and vocal cords replicated with the use of rubber and a soft batting. The movable parts of the simulated head were controlled by a variety of levers, and the vocal cords created by air passing through a slotted rubber membrane. Although the model may have looked somewhat grotesque, reminiscent of a cheap monster movie, Mr. Bell claimed that the device could speak vowels, nasals, and even, as he gained more practice, simple connected phrases. As he played the talking mechanical head, he was reminded of his earlier days when he really began to understand the physiology and mechanics of speech.

Alexander Bell, with his curiosity in the speech mechanism because of his father's voice school, had seen at his side the potential challenge of speech. It existed with all the mechanisms intact, lacking only the knowledge and creativity to speak. His pet Skye terrier was soon taught to sit up on his hind legs and growl for sustained periods of time. As his pet growled for food (and got much fatter), Bell would manipulate the throat and mouth of his pet gently to create the sounds such a limited vocal tract could articulate, The results of his efforts were a set of five sounds consisting of the vowels "ah" and "oo," the morphemes "ma" and "ga," and the diphthong "ou." Using this rather limited vocabulary and several pounds of food, Bell was said to have made his favorite pet speak the phrase "How are you, Grandmama?" It was also said that, at times, his pet with a sparkle in his eye, would attempt to say the phrase by himself but would accomplish nothing more than "grrr." Nevertheless, the trials and tribulations of young Bell in teaching his dog "to talk" had given him the insights required for the first manipulations of his mechanical talking head.

Into the 20th Century

As always, there was continued interest in the synthesis of speech based on the mechanical methods of time past. And, as the understanding of electronics dawned, there were even a few attempts at electrical analogies to the speech system. In 1922, J. Q. Stewart reported in *Nature Magazine* on his electrical analog of the vocal organs. His rather crude circuit represented in Fig. 5-2 consisted of an electrical buzzer to simulate the vocal cords, with a pair of inductive/capacitive resonators to create resonances of the throat and mouth. The resultant speech from his electrical analog, which at best could produce two formant frequencies, consisted primarily of vowel sounds. As he varied the capacitance, resistance, and inductance of the circuit components he could continuously change from one vowel sound to another, thus also creating a few diphthongs.

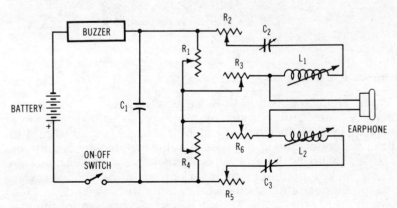

Fig. 5-2. J.Q. Stewart's voice circuit.

The availability of complex electrical components was still rather limited at this time so the quest for mechanical synthesis of speech also continued in parallel. In 1937, R. R. Riesz demonstrated his mechanical talker which, like the other mechanical devices, was more reminiscent of a musical instrument. The device was shaped like the human vocal tract and constructed primarily of rubber and metal with playing keys similar to those found on a trumpet. The mechanical talking device which produced fairly good speech with a trained operator is illustrated in Fig. 5-3. With the ten control keys (or valves) operated simultaneously with two hands, the device could produce relatively articulate speech. Riesz had, through his use of the ten keys, allowed for control of almost every movable portion of the human vocal tract. Reports from that time stated that its most articulate speech was produced as it said the word "cigarette."

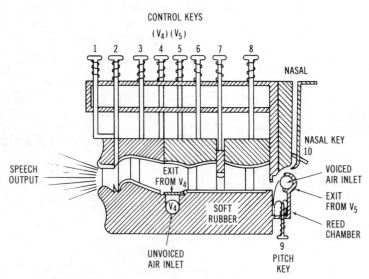

Fig. 5-3. R.R. Riesz's talking mechanism.

Almost simultaneously with Riesz's development of the "trumpet key" mechanical talker, he also worked with the development of one of the first truly electrical speech synthesizers to produce connected speech. As with his mechanical system, he created (with the help of H. W. Dudley and S. A. Watkins) an electrical-keyboard-operated-speaking system which was eventually demonstrated at the world's fairs in New York in 1939 and in San Francisco in 1940. A schematic diagram of the machine known as the "Voder" is shown in Fig. 5-4. It consisted of electrical generators to simulate voiced and unvoiced speech. These were followed by a resonance control system consisting of ten parallel connected bandpass filters which covered the entire audio spectrum. Ten piano-type keys were linked through variable resistors or potentiometers to control each of the ten bandpass filters. A wrist bar was provided for selection of the voiced or unvoiced speech control, and pitch variation came from the foot operated pedal. Other piano-type keys were also provided to produce the stop consonants and silence.

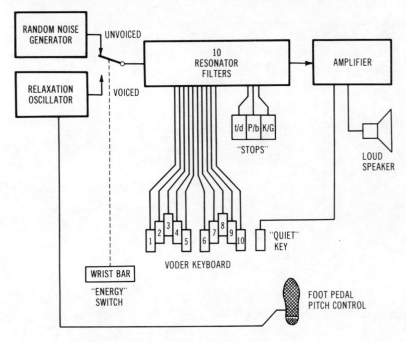

Fig. 5-4. The 1939 World's Fair Voder synthesizer.

Visitors to the world's fairs saw the operator—trained on the machine for at least a year—playing the speaking system like a trained organist or pianist. Speech from this system was said to have been quite excellent. The quality was obviously suitable for demonstration at a world's fair.

The construction of the Voder is very similar in principle to that of the phonetic speech synthesis systems in use today. What has been done in these systems is the substitution of the keyboard controls with computer output ports which simplifies our skill needed for programming the system. Further research since the Voder into synthetic speech has been concerned with computer-generated speech, and basically falls under one of the three major categories of speech synthesis methods: reconstructed speech, phonetic synthesized speech, and mathematically synthesized speech.

Since these speech technologies are considered to be in the realm of today's techniques, we will move out of the historical review and into the state-of-the-art descriptions given in the next chapter.

chapter   6

A Closer Look
at Today's Techniques

Well, this is it! The chapter you've been waiting for. Now that you've been introduced to the fundamentals for speech generation and synthesis in the previous five chapters, you should be ready to plunge into the subject of electronic speech synthesis. This chapter on the techniques of current speech synthesis activity, because of its complex nature, will be one of the longest in this book. However, by the time you have finished this chapter, you should have a complete understanding of the methods of speech synthesis and the means by which these methods are implemented. Although some of the more obscure techniques for generating artificial speech may be unintentionally omitted, the major types of computer generation of synthetic speech in existence today are thoroughly investigated.

There are three fundamental types of speech generation available for use by the scientist *and* home computerist. These are in order of increasing complexity·

1. The waveform encoder for direct speech reconstruction
2. The analog formant synthesizer for phonetic speech synthesis
3. Mathematical reconstruction of speech from the frequency domain such as linear predictive coded (LPC) synthesizers.

We will, in this chapter, examine these technologies in considerable detail so that you may better understand the capabilities and limitations of each method. As you become more familiar with each of the current techniques described in this chapter, you will begin to understand the differences among the variety of speech synthesizers available today. If you see a particular technique that tweaks your curiosity, then you may decide that this is the way to approach the speech synthesis challenge. On the other hand, if you are simply looking for a reliable means of voice output for your computer, then you will find in this chapter the most efficient technique for your needs. With those thoughts in mind, let's get going on one of the fastest moving areas of electronics technology today: speech synthesis. Hold on to your hats!

The Trinity of Speech Technology

As mentioned previously in this book, there are three basic methods of speech synthesis. Did you ask yourself "Why three?" Those of you with an inquisitive mind might look at the field of speech synthesis as a unified field of technology and question the need for exactly three. Why not two, four, eight, or ten?

There are a number of ways to answer these questions, none of them easy. A passable answer to the previous muses might be to compare the methods of speech synthesis with modes of transportation. For example, if we are talking about transportation, then I might say that there are three basic types of automobiles: the regular car or sedan, the sports car, and the all-terrain vehicle. Each of the classes of automobiles accomplishes the same purpose in moving you from one place to another. The primary differences between them are the style in which they do it, the cost, and speed of the trip. Each of the transportation modes has advantages and drawbacks. However, the end result is always the same. You start out at location A and you end up at location B. The analogy to speech synthesis methods may be rather abstract in this comparison, but each of the three methods of synthetic speech generation accomplishes one purpose: the output of speech from your computer. The means by which you do it, whether waveform encoding/reconstruction, phonetic formant synthesis, or mathematical reconstruction of speech depends upon the style in which you wish to generate speech, the cost of your equipment, and the speed that your voice synthesis and computer system works. Each of these synthesizer capabilities in turn provides varying degrees of understandability and speech quality. In other words, the most accurate reason that the three methods exist is that each has tradeoffs. One may produce more articulate speech while costing much more. Another may be inexpensive but have a more limited speech capability.

SPEECH SYNTHESIS "TACHOMETER"

A visual comparison of each of the types of systems available is given in Fig. 6-1. The speech synthesis "tachometer" gives the general relationship of computer speeds needed for each of the three major categories of synthetic speech generation. While the speeds shown do not present significant problems for most home computers available today, the implications of the sampling speed in bits per second relate directly to the amount of memory needed for speech storage. If we form a comparative index for the three methods of speech to compare required memory usage, then the "tachometer" becomes much more relevant to our problem of speech storage.

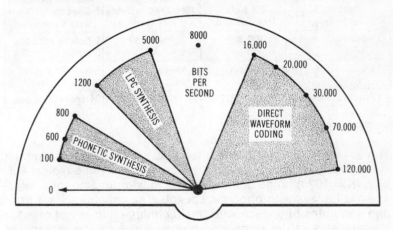

Fig. 6-1. A speech synthesis tachometer.

For instance, assume that the basic home computer has a capability of eight bits per byte in its memory storage area (most do). Since the speech "tachometer" is in bits per second, then the amount of memory storage required for each second of speech may be found by dividing the speed of each technique by eight. Now assume that we would like to test each speech technique for efficiency in storing a word such as "hello." The amount of time required to speak "hello" varies depending on your speech pattern but an appropriate measure of time might be 0.3 second. As shown in Table 6-1, which compares the three primary techniques in terms of the storage required to speak this word, the efficiency varies drastically. Each synthesis technique given in the figure has a bit rate variation over which that technique may be used. The lower bit rate in each case corresponds to relatively poor speech with a corresponding loss of intelligibility. The higher bit rate for each of the three techniques would correspond to a very articulate system having a speech quality approaching that of normal human speech. The third column, which shows the required storage (in bytes) to speak the word "hello," varies from four bytes for relatively low quality phonetic speech to 4500 bytes in the direct waveform coded storage for high quality speech. Of course, the lower quantity for each synthesis technique has approximately the same intelligibility while the upper limits for each technique provide almost perfect speech output.

Table 6-1. Comparison of Synthetic Speech Techniques

Synthesis Technique	Bit Rate Per Second	Storage Required In Bytes for "Hello"	Amount of Total Speech in 48K Byte Computer
Phonetic	100-800	4 to 30	1 hour 4 min. to 8 min.
LPC	1200-5000	45 to 188	5 min. 20 sec. to 1 min. 17 sec.
Waveform Coding	16,000-120,000	600 to 4500	24 sec. to 3.2 sec.

SPEECH STORAGE

The column in Table 6-1 that affects us with the greatest impact is the total amount of speech storage capability in a typical 48K byte (K = 1024) home computer. The maximum amount of storage available is with phonetic speech. The capability for 1 hour and 4 minutes of speech with this technique allows not only for storage of a rather large vocabulary, but also the storage of other programs to drive the speaking system. As we look at the other end of the technique spectrum, the fastest and least efficient of the synthesis techniques, waveform coding, will store only 3.2 seconds of intelligible speech in the entire memory of the 48K home computer.

Remember that these memory requirements are only for the speech storage. Your memory should also include the vocabulary that you wish to speak. For example, if you would like to have a 100-word vocabulary from which to create random sentences and phrases, and you assume that each word in your vocabulary would take approximately one-half second to speak, then you have a minimum of 50 seconds of speech storage required before you begin the creation of sentences. Now if we take that number and again look at Table 6-1, we see that the waveform coding technique would allow a maximum of 48 words (24 seconds) in our vocabulary with *no* room left for other speech phrase programming. The solution to such a problem might be to store the speech vocabulary directly as phrases without the capability for random word access and then call up each phrase as needed. This would limit us to a much smaller speaking vocabulary but possibly provide room for the speech driving programs which obviously must coexist in memory.

The previous comparison of the speech output techniques does not attempt to provide a decision or judgment on any of the techniques. It is given to illustrate the capabilities and limitations of each method. The choice of how you wish to approach the synthetic speech capability is up to you. Chapter 7 gives an overview of many of the available systems on the market today with approximate costs. While reviewing these systems in Chapter 7, remember the speech synthesis tachometer and associated storage requirements for each synthesis method.

Computer Synthetic Speech

One last point to consider in comparing the three methods for generating synthetic speech is the definition of "synthetic speech." From this, there can be at least two basic arguments as to whether speech from a computer truly represents *synthetic speech.*

The first argument says that for a computer to generate truly "synthetic" speech, the words which are spoken by the computer should not have been prespoken by a human for ultimate memory storage. The analogy to a digital or electronic memory "tape" recorder is most accurate to this argument. If, in fact, the words or phrases to be spoken by your computer have been "prespoken" by a person, whether by yourself or in an integrated circuit manufacturing facility, then the speech you are using is reconstructed speech. Two methods of reconstructed speech exist in the speech "tachometer." These are the direct waveform coding method and the LPC synthesis method. While these two synthetic speech principles differ greatly in their implementation, they both generally require a prespoken vocabulary for ultimate speech regeneration. What this analysis shows is that the phonetic speech synthesis method is the only truly synthetic speech method. Of course, it also means that the phonetic speech synthesis method sounds less human than the other two. In fact, with today's technology, the reconstructed speech methods are the only ones which generate speech that is pleasing to our ears. The truly "synthetic" speech from the phoneme synthesizer is relatively robotic in its sound. In other words, if you desire *real* synthetic speech, then you should expect your computer to sound like a Cylon warrior from the beginning. If you opt for one of the reconstructed speech methods, then you have a system which sounds pleasing to the ear and approaches normal human articulation.

The second argument for the meaning of synthetic speech is related to the basic sampling theory of data acquisition. Many years ago a scientist named Henry Nyquist of Bell Labs determined that to adequately sample and store a representative analog signal or waveform, the sampling rate should be at least twice the highest frequency component in the sampled waveform. An example of this sampling theorem would be illustrated as follows. If you wish to sample a voice signal with a maximum frequency content of around 4 kHz, then your sampling rate on this signal should be at least 8 kHz or higher. And, with each sample, the value or amplitude of the waveform should also be stored. This would require at least four bits for relatively understandable reproduction. So the product of the four bits times the 8 kHz sampling rate is a bit sampling rate of approximately 32,000 bits per second. Since some redundancy exists in speech, and marginally intelligible speech can be reproduced with a 2 kHz maximum frequency content, this sampling rate at the very least should be 16,000 bits per second. This is shown in the speech tachometer in Fig. 6-1. If by some means we could reconstruct the same quality speech with a lower than expected reconstruction rate of 16,000 bits per second, then we are no longer reproducing digitally reconstructed speech. So this is a second possible definition of synthetic speech. Under this definition the phonetic synthesis and LPC synthesis methods become truly synthetic speech. For that matter, any speech output system which operates at a bit rate lower than 16,000 bits per second would be considered to be synthesized. No matter how the term is ultimately defined, the capabilities of each, with their tradeoffs, all serve to produce speech output from your computer. In this light, the arguments become irrelevant. Whichever method best suits your computer and pocketbook is the one for you. Now let's examine each of the technologies of these major synthesis methods in more detail.

The Waveform Encoding/Reconstruction Technique

This simplest method of speech generation most closely resembles the digital recorder. The concept of sampling of analog signals for later speech reconstruction was introduced earlier. The understanding of the sampling mechanism is paramount to the understanding of speech encoding/reconstruction techniques. If you have any difficulty in understanding the concept of analog signal sampling, then let me illustrate an example for you. For this experiment, we will pick visual sampling. The concepts involved are identical; the only difference is that the analog signal is visual rather than aural.

The first thing that you should do is to find an active scene such as the television screen or a nearby expressway over which cars are moving rapidly. Now watch that scene and close your eyes. If you will momentarily open your eyes much like that of a movie camera shutter about one time per second, you should have no difficulty in describing the motion and action in the scene you are viewing. Continue to blink your eyes open for several seconds to see that you can, in fact, follow the action and sequence of events that are occurring before your eyes. This corresponds to a visual sampling of the motion (analog signal) that you are watching. If something should occur very rapidly while you were blinking your eyes at a one-time-per-second rate, then you would simply miss that action. This can be further illustrated by lowering the blinking rate of your eyes to approximately one time per ten seconds. If you close your eyes and count to ten, then momentarily open your eyes and repeat this for a minute or two, you will realize that you can describe very little of the sequence of events that you are watching. What you have done, in effect, is to lower your sampling rate below the Nyquist criteria for observing and describing adequately the analog signal that you are watching. If you, on the other hand, blink your eyes very rapidly while watching the scene, then you should have no trouble at all in following and describing the action you are watching. This example is a direct analogy to the concept of sampled audio speech except one is visual, the other electronic. As we begin to discuss the waveform encoding/reconstruction technique in light of the previous example, we find very few differences. Once the speech signal has been converted to electrical signals by a microphone, the resultant waveform has relatively slow moving and extremely fast moving components within it. If we were to sample the waveform at a relatively slow rate, then the best observations we could make on that signal are that the slower components do exist. The high speed components of the signal would be lost to our sampling inquiry. As we begin to sample the electrical speech signal from the microphone at a faster and faster rate, we start to see the higher frequencies that exist within the signal. Consider, for example, the comparison of sampling frequencies given in Fig. 6-2.

The input signal at the top of this figure represents the analog waveform to be sampled by our digital sampling system. It corresponds to a complex waveform much like that found in speech processing. If you will examine the signal closely you will notice that there are slowly varying portions and rapidly varying portions on the same signal. In terms of spectral content, the slowly varying signals would represent the lower frequency components while the rapidly varying signal in the center of the waveform corresponds to a higher frequency content. As we begin to sample the signal, which occurs during a 5 millisecond window, at a sampling rate of one sample per millisecond, the resultant pulse amplitude modulated signal shown in Fig. 6-2A gives relatively little information about the original waveform. If you were to try to reconstruct the original signal given these five pulses, you would be able only to reconstruct the lowest frequency components. If we double the sampling rate to twice per millisecond, then we have the resultant sampled data given in Fig. 6-2B. Notice that in this sampled data a slight amount more information is available about the original input signal. As we continue to double the sampling rate in Fig. 6-2C and again in Fig. 6-2D, the pulse amplitude modulated signal which results from the sampling process begins to resemble the data with more fidelity. This process could be carried on with a repeated doubling of the sampling fre-

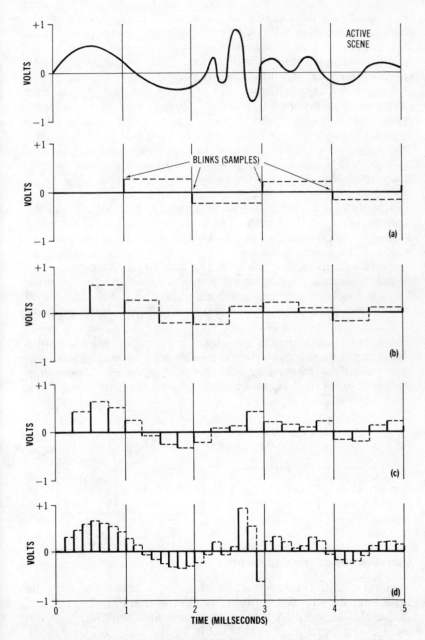

Fig. 6-2. An increasing signal sampling rate.

quency until the waveform is so accurately represented that additional sampling speed no longer adds to the quality of the sampled data. Since the highest frequency component within the original active scene (analog input) waveform occurs in slightly under one-half millisecond, the Nyquist sampling theorem tells us we should be able to adequately characterize the signal by sampling at a rate of four times per millisecond. This would correspond to Fig. 6-2C. And, in fact, this waveform does capture most of the higher frequency undulations of the signal. To ensure high fidelity reproduction of the signal, the sampling rate could be doubled to eight times per millisecond as shown in Fig. 6-2D. The signal would then be captured relatively undistorted.

The process of sampling an analog signal as previously shown yields a sampled data train of analog pulses having a height or amplitude of the signal at the time it was sampled, and the width of the sampling pulse. This type of information would be very difficult to store directly in the memory of a computer. In order to store the sampled data values, we must first digitize the waveform in terms of amplitude variations. An example of how this might be done is shown in Fig. 6-3 in block diagram form.

The speech sampling system shown in Fig. 6-3 takes the sound information from a microphone and initially passes it through a low pass filter to remove the speech frequency components above one-half the sampling rate. This is done to prevent the

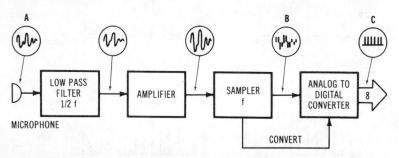

Fig. 6-3. A speech sampling system.

aliasing of data produced when sampling at less than twice the frequency component content (remember Nyquist). The second stage of the sampling system is an amplifier which brings the level of the signal to a usable value for the sampler. Of course, the sampler performs the same process on the signal as shown in Fig. 6-2. Its output corresponds to a train of amplitude modulated pulses corresponding to the analog value of the signal at each sampling time. The final block within the speech sampling system (Fig. 6-3) is the analog-to-digital (a/d) converter. Notice that this box has one input line corresponding to the analog sampled voltage input, and eight output lines. More complex analog-to-digital converters exist with up to 16 or 18 bits of data output, but for our consideration of this system, 8 bits is adequate. The 8-bit output from the analog-to-digital converter is used to feed the computer input data. At this point, the input signal has gone from analog variations to digital data and exists as pulse code modulation (pcm) from the a/d converter.

The three waveforms shown in Fig. 6-3 labeled A, B, and C are emphasized in Fig. 6-4 to illustrate the pulse code modulation process. This is one example of how a speech signal goes from an analog form to a form capable of being stored in computer memory. Notice that in following the figure from A through C, the input waveform is first sampled and then converted to pulse

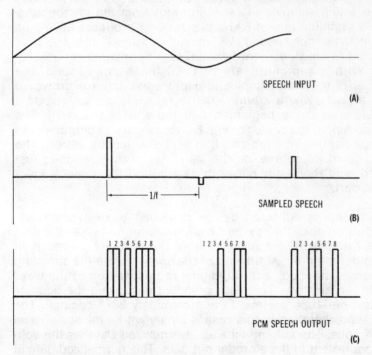

Fig. 6-4. Amplitude to pcm conversion of speech.

code modulated data. The important characteristic of Fig. 6-4C is that there are no amplitude varying signals in this data train and therefore it is ideal for computer memory storage. Each of the 8 bits in the pcm speech output could be input to a serial port of the computer for memory storage. On the other hand, the 8 parallel bits could be transferred through a parallel port and stored directly byte for byte. After the data is input and stored in the computer, then existing within memory is a digital amplitude record of the originally spoken sound. The speech data in memory can be manipulated through software to condense or pack the information to reduce memory requirements. This technique will be discussed later in this section.

So, now that we know how to sample and capture analog speech in our computer memory, what do we do with it next? Well, one possible course of action would be to construct a very simple waveform encoded synthesizer. The illustrative diagram of such a synthesizer for any home computer is shown in Fig. 6-5. Across the upper portion of this figure you will see the familiar speech sampling system as described in the previous figure which samples the speech input from the microphone. With a sampling rate of 6 kHz this sampler produces 6000 8-bit output bytes per second. We recently assumed that the time required to speak the word "hello" was approximately 0.3 second. With a sampling rate of 6000 times per second, the number of required samples to capture the entire word would then be somewhere around 2000 bytes. This would include a short pause at the beginning and the end of the word. The dashed box in the center of Fig. 6-6 represents a computer with an 8-bit parallel input port and an 8-bit parallel output port. The ports could, of course, be the same port if the speech is first stored, and then later played back through the same bidirectional port.

As the data is collected by the computer (shown within the computer block), the resident computer program takes the data from the 8-bit a/d converter and sequentially stores it in computer memory. At the end of the spoken word the sampling process is stopped, with the digital representation of the word "hello" in memory. This data is shown occupying the address space from 1024 decimal to approximately 3073 decimal. The data representation in this case is binary with a full scale value of ±5 volts. The column labeled "Normalized Data" is the voltage equivalent of the stored input data. This normalized data in volts is not really of any value to the computer, but is shown to

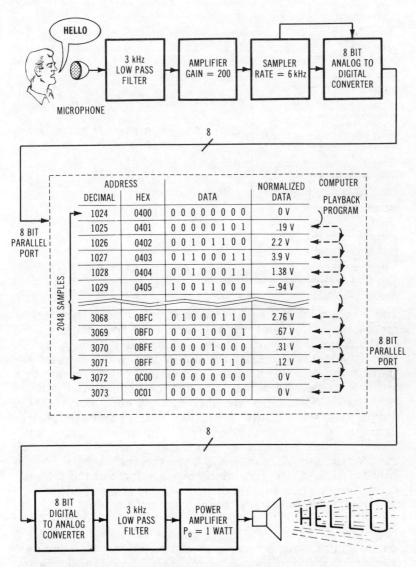

Fig. 6-5. Simplified waveform encoded speech synthesis diagram.

illustrate the equivalence of the analog-to-digital sampling process. At this point in our synthesizer diagram we have completely stored the analog speech in digital form and may save this data on a disk or cassette tape for later playback.

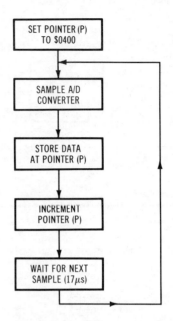

Fig. 6-6. A possible speech input program flow.

The playback portion of the waveform encoded synthesizer represents the speech output section of the diagram. The playback program which resides in computer memory during speech output is a simple indexing program which sequentially steps through the original stored data and outputs it one byte at a time to the 8-bit digital-to-analog (d/a) converter. If this d/a converter is compatible with the input a/d converter, then the normalization and conversion of the data to volts should not concern you. The converters will sequentially follow each other, producing the same output voltage that was originally sampled. All this really means is that if the original sampling a/d converter had a full scale range of ±5 volts, and the 8 bit d/a converter also has a range of ±5 volts full scale, then the output should faithfully track the original input signal.

The output from the 8-bit d/a converter is then fed through a 3 kHz low-pass filter to remove unwanted artifact high frequencies created during the signal reconstruction. (These are the square corners in Fig. 6-2D.) The output of the low-pass filter is finally amplified with a power amplifier to drive a loudspeaker with the original voice signal. The speech output from the loudspeaker should accurately represent the original speech input with a slight loss of high frequency response due to the low-pass filters. Otherwise the sound will represent the voice of the speaker and have the original cadence and tonality of its input.

The only thing missing from the speech synthesizer diagram in Fig. 6-5 is the method of speech storage used within the computer during signal acquisition, and the playback program used during voice synthesis. Because of the rather high sampling rate of 6 kHz, the computer has only approximately 17 microseconds to acquire and store each byte of data in memory. This requirement for computer speed eliminates the possible use of a BASIC or other high level language program to acquire and play back speech data. So you have only one means of acquiring and playing back the synthesized speech: assembly language programs. A flowchart of one possible speech acquisition program is given in Fig. 6-6 to illustrate the simplicity of the speech encoding process. Once the data is in memory, a playback program may be executed to reproduce the originally encoded speech. The simplicity of this assembly language type program is shown in Fig. 6-7 which is a reversal of the previous program flow in Fig. 6-6. The only critical similarity between these programs is that the output program retain the same equivalent sampling rate of the original input program. In other words, if each input sample occurs at a rate of 6000 times per

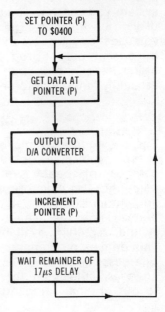

Fig. 6-7. A simple speech playback program flow.

second, then you certainly want your output rate to the d/a converter to also occur at 6000 times per second. If these sampling rates are different, then the speech you hear from the system will have a different sound than the original, much like playing a 45 rpm record at 33⅓ rpm or vice versa.

This is also one way of creating some rather unusual sound effects from your computer by changing the last block in Fig. 6-7 to a slower or faster delay time. If you leave this block out and your program executes in under 17 microseconds per loop, then your output speech will begin to sound like Donald Duck. If you were to place within this block a delay of more than 17 microseconds, then your speech will begin to sound like a slow motion grumble. What you are effectively doing if you experiment with the delay block is a time expansion or compression of your original input speech. It might seem to you that your normal voice would appear to speed up or slow down while retaining all the original frequencies. On the contrary, if you double the playback delay from 17 microseconds to 34 microseconds, then you have effectively lowered all of your voice frequencies to one-half of their original values. So, if you attempt this simple voice encoding/reconstruction synthesizer project and succeed in getting a voice playback with an *improper* pitch, then go straight to the delay block in Fig. 6-7 and change it until your voice sounds correct. With this simple system you can have many hours of enjoyment recording and playing back speech and other sounds from your computer. If you use the system creatively, then you could possibly integrate the speech output program with games and other BASIC programs (remember though that the playback program must be in assembly language) to create speech from your computer.

Delta Modulation

The previous example of waveform encoded/reconstructed speech synthesis is not, by any means, the only method in this category of speech synthesis. Several other methods have come into use which provide more efficient ways of digitizing and storing the voice signal. One of these, which is in considerable use in the telephone industry and some of the speech synthesizer chips available today, is called *delta modulation*. This primary difference between this process and the previous one described in Fig. 6-5 is that it relies on *relative amplitude changes* rather than absolute amplitude values. If we go back to our original sampling analogy of an automobile traveling along a road, then we might understand how this delta modulation technique works. Using the previously described technique with parallel byte encoding, we would describe a trip from point A to point B during each sample as:

1. The car is 100 feet from point A.
2. The car is 200 feet from point A.
3. The car is 300 feet from point A.
4. The car is 400 feet from point A.
5. The car is 500 feet from point A.

and so on. Thus, at any time we can tell where the car is in relation to its beginning. This type of absolute sampling is illustrated in Fig. 6-8. If you can imagine the path of an analog waveform resembling the path of an automobile over time, then all we have to do to correct the analogy is to change the units of feet to volts.

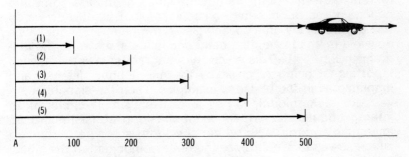

Fig. 6-8. An example of absolute sampling.

Now let's take a look at how delta modulation changes the sampling process by assuming that we are only interested in the relative change from the present sample to the previous sample. By doing so, we lose information about the absolute sampled quantity, but in a sequential signal, who cares? By eliminating this redundant information, we have increased our information storage capabilities necessary to describe the analog signal. The same automobile trip just given may be described in terms of a delta modulation as follows:

1. The car has traveled 100 feet from point A.
2. The car has traveled 100 feet since the last sample.
3. The car has traveled 100 feet since the last sample.
4. The car has traveled 100 feet since the last sample.
5. The car has traveled 100 feet since the last sample.

and so on. Now, if you were to carry this trip out to a hundred miles, then using the previous sampling method in Fig. 6-9 you would be storing numbers in the range of 500,000 feet or greater. At any sample point you would know exactly where that car was in relation to its starting point A. But during each sample, the stored quantity (of number of feet traveled) has become excessive. The illustration of delta modulation encoding in Fig. 6-9 shows the same trip described only in terms of the difference (or delta) in distance between each sampling time. Thus, even over trips of hundreds of miles, the largest number that needs to be stored in memory to describe this trip is 100 feet since the last sample. Obviously the memory storage requirements for 100 are much less than that of 500,000. That is how delta modulation increases the efficiency of speech sampling in a rather abstract comparison of our automobile excursion.

The delta modulation process is also often referred to as an incremental encoding method because it encodes only the change of the signal between each sample. But, how do we do this electronically on a speech signal from a microphone? One possible method of digital delta encoding is shown in the diagram in Fig. 6-10. This electronic diagram shows the speech input signal being received by the microphone, filtered, and amplified as in the previous examples. Then the signal is converted to delta modulation by a relatively simple circuit of an analog comparator with a feedback loop consisting of an analog integrator. Also within the loop is a type D flip-flop which serves to synchronize the delta component of the signal (or slope change) with the digitizing clock rate. A closer look at the signals which occur during the delta encoding process is shown in Fig. 6-11. Notice that the input signal at the top is an

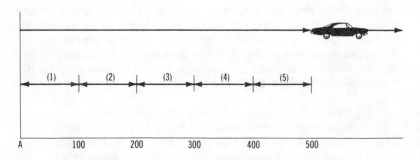

Fig. 6-9. An example of delta modulation encoding.

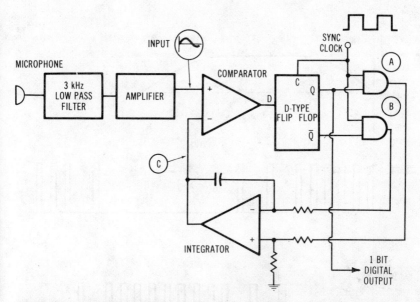

Fig. 6-10. An electronic delta encoding method.

oscillating waveform which has both rising slopes and falling slopes and periods of *signal stability*. The gated outputs from the D type flip-flop of Fig. 6-10 are represented by signals A and B in Fig. 6-11 that are constant value 5-volt pulses used to feed the integrator whose output is signal C. The signal changes are sampled at each of the sample periods identified as the time period T in waveform A. If the input waveform continues to rise, then the pulses at point A indicate a continuously increasing input signal. The waveforms at point B indicate a falling input signal. During the period of time when the signal remains at a fixed value, then the delta modulator goes into an oscillation around the voltage value by alternately pulsing both lines A and B. The signal output at point C is the feedback signal compared with the input signal from the integrator. The last signal in Fig. 6-11 is the digital output from the system to your computer. This single bit value is stored in computer memory at the same clock sampling rate used in the delta encoder in Fig. 6-10.

Reconstruction of the delta encoded signal requires even simpler hardware to provide adequate sound reproduction. The diagram shown in Fig. 6-12 is a simple integrator much like that used in the encoding process. The input E to the integrator is a single logic bit from the computer at the digitized rate of the

97

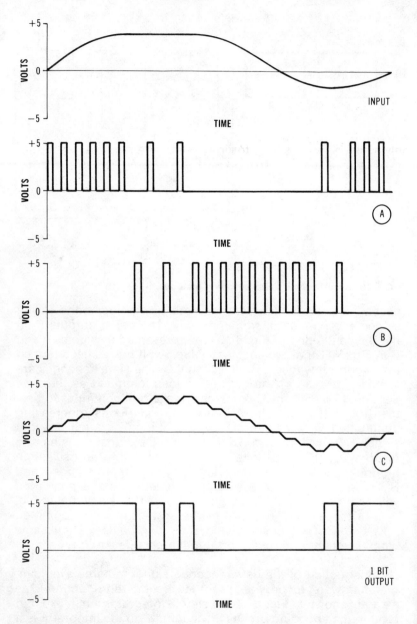

Fig. 6-11. The delta encoding signals.

98

digital sampling process. The time constant of the integrator which is represented by the R X C_T product is set to match the original integration time of the sampling system. If the input bit to the playback circuit is a logic 1, then the integrator continues to produce a constant slope in one direction. As the input bit changes to a logic 0, then the same integrator reverses its output slope to the opposite polarity. This results in an equivalent signal to that found at point F. The waveform shown in Fig. 6-12 as F shows the reproduction of the original input signal through delta modulation. As you can see, the waveform is a fairly good representation of the original with only a slight amount of distortion added. The amount of encoding distortion generated by the delta modulation process is generally due to an encoding distortion known as slope overload. If the input slope changes faster than the integrators can track, then the output simply can't keep up with the input

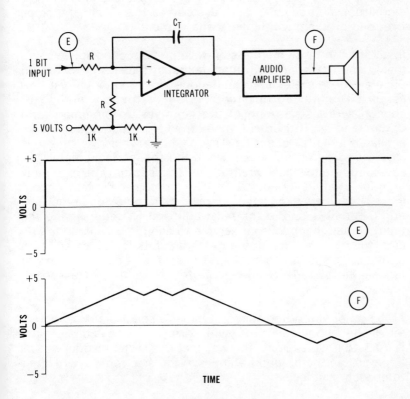

Fig. 6-12. Delta encoded speech playback circuit.

changes. This problem, which is inherent in linear delta modulation, can be overcome by utilizing an offshoot of this modulation technique known as adaptive delta pulse code modulation (adpcm). This method of encoding is used by several synthetic chip manufacturers, including the National Digitalker™ Speech Synthesis System.

The adaptive pulse code modulation system is very similar to the linear system with the exception of storing not only a slope change since the last sample, but also the amount of the change since the last sample. By doing this, the advantages of the previous system are still maintained and the slope overload problem is eliminated. To put it very simply, instead of using a single bit to represent whether the signal slope is rising or falling, four bits can be used to indicate whether the slope is rising or falling with a slope description of eight possible levels for each rising or falling condition. This more accurately describes the change in the signal between samples and also serves to prevent the slope overload problem with linear delta modulation.

In addition to these methods of waveform encoded speech synthesis, there are several other methods that are used but, in general, these systems are mutations of the methods just presented. The waveform encoding/reconstruction method of speech synthesis is one of the simplest to implement and understand. As previously mentioned, the technique is very similar to a digital recording. The means by which the speech is stored may differ but, as shown in the speech tachometer, the sampling rate for these methods must necessarily be extremely high for true fidelity output. Of the methods of digitally encoding a speech waveform the adaptive delta pulse code modulation (adpcm) is one of the most efficient. By representing the input signal changes from sample to sample with a slope and amplitude value, the number of storage bits for each sample is reduced. This is the point of speech synthesis research: how to reduce the storage requirements for the output of a spoken phrase.

At the other end of the speech synthesis spectrum or tachometer is the phoneme driven synthesizer using analog formant synthesis. If we examine the way that this system works we will begin to see the great differences in the electronic approaches to speech synthesis.

---

*Digitalker is a trademark of National Semiconductor Corp.

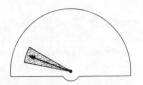

Analog Formant Frequency Speech Synthesis

The previously described waveform encoded/reconstructed speech may be considered a "photograph" of human speech. The technique of analog formant frequency speech synthesis, on the other hand, might be considered an oil painting of the same speech. In the previous section, waveform encoded speech must exist prior to be spoken by the synthesizer, much like a scene must exist to be photographed. In contrast, the formant synthesis method is man's interpretation of the same speech like oil on a canvas. The esthetics of the two methods of speech synthesis are very similar to those of the two methods of imagery: the photograph is a reproduction of the original, while the oil painting is very close to the original but will never quite be the same. But, depending on the desired effect, either will describe the original scene or speech.

There are numerous methods by which the realization of the formant frequency synthesis may be accomplished. However, the general functions that are used to generate this type of speech synthesis are basically the same. All methods are based upon an intimate knowledge of the phonemes and phonetic breakdown of English speech as described in Chapter 3. If we briefly continue our observations on phonetic speech in terms of quantitative values, then we can begin to lay the groundwork for understanding the formant method of speech synthesis. If you remember the description of the spectrograms of speech given in the latter part of Chapter 2 in Figs. 2-10 and 2-11, you should remember the description of the dark frequency bands of the visible speech being referred to as formant frequencies. The fact that we can visually and electronically recognize these varying formant frequencies in human speech allows us to formulate a method for creating synthetic speech based on the simultaneous generation of the necessary formant frequencies.

If you will now examine Table 6-2 while remembering the description of vowel phonemes given in Chapter 3, you will see some of the same phoneme sounds given in a more descriptive manner. The table describes the three major formant frequencies which appear when an average male voice speaks the vowels. These frequencies, F_1, F_2, and F_3, can be visibly discerned by viewing a spectrogram of each spoken vowel. Since each of these vowels are continuants, the frequencies are stable during the entire utterance. Now, if we can use a little imagination and visualize an electronic circuit with three separate bandpass filters (each centered on one of the formant frequencies, F_1, F_2, or F_3), being excited by an oscillator having a waveform similar to the glottal pulse, then we have the system in Fig. 6-13. As simple as this figure seems, it can form a basic phoneme synthesizer of vowels if the frequencies F_1, F_2, and F_3 are adjustable over the ranges given in Table 6-2.

Table 6-2. Typical Formant Frequencies of Some Vowel Phonemes

Phoneme	"as in"	F_1	F_2	F_3
ee	feet	250	2300	3000
i	hid	375	2150	2800
eh	head	550	1950	2600
ae	had	700	1800	2550
ah	tot	775	1100	2500
aw	talk	575	900	2450
u	took	425	1000	2400
oo	tool	275	850	2400

During operation, the center frequency of each of the parallel bandpass filters is adjusted to match the equivalent resonance of the mouth and throat cavities during speech. The speech output that results from the summation of the filter outputs very closely resembles human speech. A spectrogram of the output signal from this circuit would have three formant frequencies existing identically as in the human speech spectrogram of the same vowels. If we replaced the four manual adjustments in Figure 6-13 with computer controls for glottal pitch and the three formant frequencies, then we should be able to program our computer to speak the vowels on our command. This is the basis for the analog formant frequency speech synthesis system.

The only problem we have now with our analog formant synthesizer is that we are limited strictly to vowel sounds. While this might make an interesting demonstration system for illustrating how phonetic speech can be electronically generated, you would quickly run out of complete words or phrases that

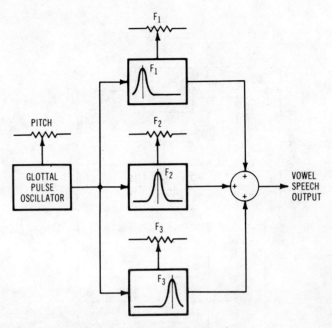

Fig. 6-13. An elementary formant speech synthesizer.

your system could speak. To extend the performance range of our formant synthesizer, we must add the noise source to produce the fricative and stop consonants and a nasal resonator to simulate the nasal consonants. A block diagram of the expanded formant synthesizer is given in Figure 6-14.

The complexity difference from the previous figure is quite noticeable as we add the remainder of the capabilities for complete speech synthesis. However, the complexity is not that much greater. Notice that instead of four controls, there are now nine. Three of these are amplitude controls for the fricative, voiced, and nasal sounds; one is the glottal pitch and the remaining five are for the various resonator frequency adjustments. If such a system were constructed having nine knobs on the front panel and you had extremely fast moving hands, then you might be able to reproduce speech from this system much like the early pioneers "played" their historical speaking machines. Fortunately, we have the advantage of computer control over these various adjustments to help with our synthetic speech generation (pun intended). The replacement of each of the nine adjustment potentiometers in Fig. 6-14 with parallel

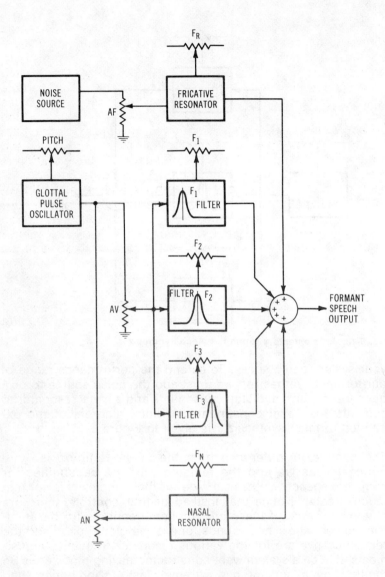

Fig. 6-14. A complete formant speech synthesizer.

computer port connections allows us to program the synthesizer at our leisure. We can then later play back the necessary
adjustments at a rate of speed adequate to approximate a normal human speech pattern.

104

Now, if we assume that we can adequately synthesize the formant frequency changes required for diphthongs and non-continuant phonemes with a complete synthesizer control updating rate of approximately 100 times per second, and each control word consists of an 8-bit byte, then we should be able to control the synthesizer with a parallel data rate of 900 bytes per second. This rate is not, however, the phoneme rate which will eventually be used by you, the user. This is the internal data rate of the synthesizer for updating all of the filter, pitch, and amplitude adjustments for each phoneme. This information is typically stored within a control table in computer memory for each phoneme and associated allophone and called up in sequence depending upon the phoneme input string from your speech output driving program. So, for instance, for each phoneme that you input to the computer, the computer control of the synthesizer may require up to 30 complete updates of the filter system. This means that for your computer to output 900 bytes per second to the control circuits within the formant synthesizer, you need only provide 30 bytes per second to the lookup table program which drives the synthesizer. This would correspond to a final user data rate of approximately 240 bits per second.

While the numbers previously cited for the filter updating rate may vary from system to system, the relationship of the phoneme-to-control table size will be approximately the same. Of course, the higher the ratio of lookups for each phoneme, the smoother the speech will sound and more closely approximate normal human articulation. But, don't think that this system will ever sound completely human. Because its speech is truly synthesized speech, there is a robotic sound which characterizes most people's thought of computer speech. This effect can be very impressive if you are demonstrating the system to your friends, but they may have trouble understanding the resultant speech output. There is no way, however, that anyone could ever imagine that the speech that they were hearing from a phoneme-driven analog formant synthesizer was prerecorded or reconstructed speech. It *is* computer speech!

Let's take a look at how a computer might handle the excitation functions for a typical phoneme-driven formant frequency speech synthesizer. One configuration for the control of such a speaking system is shown in Fig. 6-15. At the left is a computer which may be of your choosing. The primary characteristics that a computer must have to drive this system are:

1. an array of 8-bit output ports to drive the various control functions,
2. a single 8-bit input port to notify the computer that the synthesizer is ready for the next updating frame.

As you follow the various control lines from the top to the bottom of this figure, you should recognize the familiar controls needed for the formant synthesizer shown in Figure 6-14. The *busy* signal lines at the bottom of the figure indicate to the computer when the formant speech synthesizer is finished speaking a data frame. This terminology (a data frame) signifies that the synthesizer is not driven randomly through each of the ports. Instead, the computer updates all of the nine parallel output ports simultaneously for a given phoneme or portion of the phoneme, waits for the completion of that spoken frame (typically about 33 milliseconds long), and then continues the cycle of complete control updating.

The functional computer program flow of a typical formant synthesis program is shown in Fig. 6-16. If we assume that the word "hello" is to be spoken, then the program must first parse (break into individual component phonemes) the input word "hello." For sake of simplicity, let's assume that the word can be crudely spoken with the four phonemes "h," "eh," "l," and "o." If you really attempted to speak the word "hello" from this string of phonemes, the sound would be very harsh to your ears and probably not very understandable. Most phoneme synthesizers have such a variety of phonemes and allophones available for speech generation that seven or eight phonemic sounds would be used to more accurately speak the word "hello."

As we continue to follow the flowchart through the speech output process, we see that the computer accesses a control table for each phoneme to be spoken. If this is a continuant phoneme, then the phoneme control table (which might be nine bytes wide by 30 update frames long) might have the same update frame repeated 30 times. One of the noncontinuant phonemes or diphthongs would have a set of changing update frames for each control table because of the dynamic properties of that spoken sound. As the computer accesses each of these update frames and outputs them to the speech synthesizer output ports, the system begins to speak. When the speech synthesizer completes a spoken update frame, it signals the computer that it is no longer *busy* speaking and the

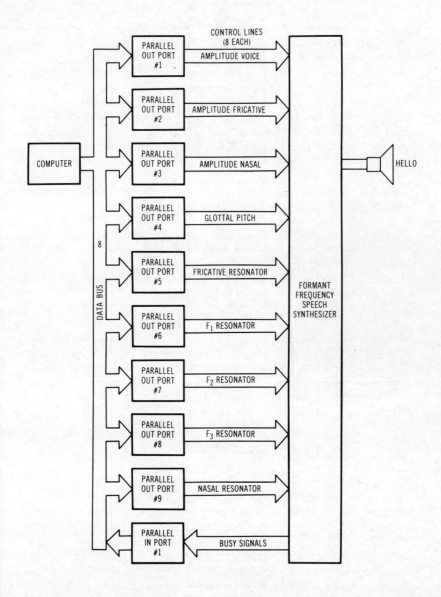

Fig. 6-15. A possible computer-driven formant frequency speech synthesizer.

107

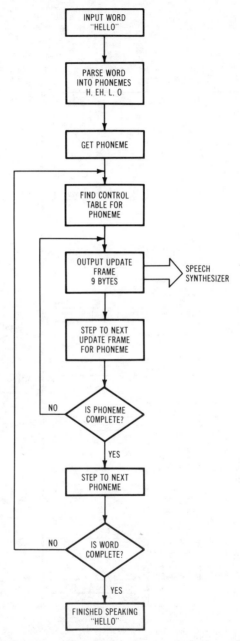

Fig. 6-16. A program flow for a formant frequency phoneme synthesizer.

computer steps through the control table for the next update frame for the phoneme being spoken. At the completion of each phoneme in succession the computer program steps to the next phoneme in the spoken word and begins to repeat the above cycle. This continues until all of the individual phonemes of the parsed word have been spoken. The system is then ready for the next input word in the connected speech utterance.

That's all there is to it. Seems simple enough, doesn't it? Or does it? If you stopped during the software flow for that driving program at the block "Find Control Table for Phoneme" and conjured up a mental blank, then don't worry. The manufacturers of these formant synthesis systems have been considerate enough to supply the phoneme control tables within the resident memory of the speaking peripherals. In fact, if you tried to find these control tables within the speech synthesis systems, you probably couldn't because they are usually considered proprietary to the operation of each system. What you get instead is a single input port for supplying the sequence of phonemes for the speech utterance. In some cases, as in the Votrax Type 'N Talk™* formant synthesizer, the phoneme parsing function is even included within the speech system. This means that you only have to input the English word to the system for correct pronunciation. All of the logic within Fig. 6-16 is performed within the speech synthesis peripheral. This capability also exists within some of the linear predictive coding (LPC) phoneme and allophone synthesizers to be described within the next section. The flow with phonetic LPC is generally the same except that the speech filters being controlled are digital rather than analog.

Phoneme and allophone driven synthesizers have the capability for speaking an unlimited vocabulary because of their design. Since these types of synthesizers speak sequential sounds which are found in normal human speech, all you have to do to speak any word is correctly string the sounds of that word together. The number of sounds or phonemes which phoneme synthesizers employ varies from manufacturer to manufacturer. Some rather crude synthesizers have only 32 available phonemes, while others supply the user with the capability for hundreds of phonemes and allophones. Obviously, the more variation of speech sounds that are available to the user, the better the final connected phonemes will sound. At the same

---

*Type 'N Talk is a trademark of Votrax Div. of Federal Screw Works

time, however, the data rate for speech is increasing as are the memory requirements. This also puts more of a burden on the computer user if he has to phonetically parse a word.

In the previous example, the word "hello" was spoken with the four phonemes shown. An allophonic synthesizer with a very high quality speech output might require ten or fifteen varying speech sounds to articulate the diphthongs and speech dynamics occurring during a spoken word. It might be relatively easy to find the four basic sounds of the word "hello," but try to find the 14 and 15 allophones needed for the more complex systems. This becomes almost impossible for longer words. You usually end up creating the final speech by hours of trial and error in front of a keyboard.

A final observation on phoneme-driven formant speech synthesizers, might be that the more speech sounds available to the user, the better the final output speech will sound *if* you spend the time to correctly piece together the proper phonemes and allophones. If you are satisfied with the sound of fewer phonemes for the same word, then you really don't need hundreds of phonemic possibilities. All you are really doing as you add each of the additional speech sounds to the basic word is making your synthesizer more understandable to a larger and larger group of untrained listeners. So consider that. Of course, if you decide to acquire a phoneme-driven speech synthesis system with a text-to-speech capability, then remember that you are limited by the vocabulary supplied in the synthesizer's parsing table. You may still speak words outside of the table if you create the phonetic concatenates yourself. As a rule of thumb, you can generally speak only one or two sentences from a text-to-speech synthesizer before the system runs across a word that it incorrectly parses, and you have Martian talk within your speech. This is not really a fault of the speech system, but rather a result of the tremendous inconsistencies in the rules of English speech.

Analog Formant Speech Frequency Synthesizers

The analog formant speech frequency synthesis method is quite unique. If you listen to other types of speech synthesis and compare them with the formant type of synthesizer, you will have no difficulty in telling them apart. The typical formant generated speech sounds are very soft and even somewhat mushy. The early systems, using the analog formant filters, sounded like a person who was talking with a mouth full of bread. As the capabilities for control parameter variations increase within formant synthesizers, speech becomes more articulate. This is a very viable method of speech synthesis and its use will surely continue. It has the major advantage of a very slow speaking data rate as does the linear predictive coded (LPC) speech synthesis method described in the next section. Other similarities with the LPC speech synthesis technique also exist. As you review the methods of LPC speech synthesis and how the digital filtering affects the ultimate speech output, keep in mind the diagram in Fig. 6-14 for reference. You might see some striking similarities.

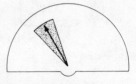

Linear Predictive Coded (LPC) Speech

Linear predictive coded speech is not only one of the most rapidly growing techniques for speech synthesis, it is also technically one of the most difficult to comprehend. This is because the regeneration of speech is done mathematically, based on the equations of the original frequency spectral content of the encoded speech. However, some similarities exist with waveform encoded/reconstructed speech methods. For instance, it would be very difficult to create LPC speech from scratch. The normal method by which the LPC parameters are generated for synthetic speech is by a person speaking the words. The similarities are so close, in fact, that if we examine the mechanism of the LPC encoding and reconstruction process, we find imbedded within it the waveform encoding process.

Fig. 6-17 shows a simplified diagram of how LPC speech is generated. At the left of this figure, there is a microphone which encodes the human speech signal into digitized speech samples through the analog-to-digital converter. The speech at this point is truly waveform encoded speech and could be stored and later reconstructed as described in the earlier section on waveform reconstructed speech. However, if instead, the speech samples are applied to a computer for digital speech analysis to determine the spectral content of the speech, we no longer have a string of digital bytes which directly resembles our input signal. The resulting output data

111

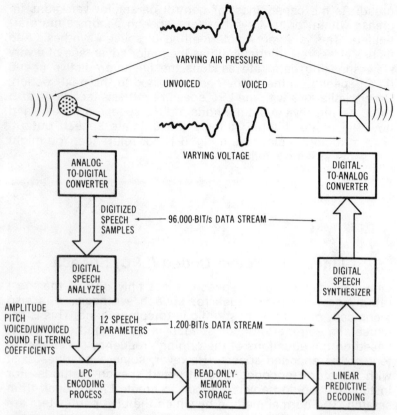

VARYING AIR PRESSURE

UNVOICED   VOICED

VARYING VOLTAGE

ANALOG-
TO-DIGITAL
CONVERTER

DIGITIZED
SPEECH
SAMPLES

← 96,000-BIT/s DATA STREAM →

DIGITAL-
TO-ANALOG
CONVERTER

DIGITAL
SPEECH
ANALYZER

AMPLITUDE
PITCH
VOICED/UNVOICED
SOUND FILTERING
COEFFICIENTS

12 SPEECH
PARAMETERS

← 1,200-BIT/s DATA STREAM →

DIGITAL
SPEECH
SYNTHESIZER

LPC
ENCODING
PROCESS

READ-ONLY-
MEMORY
STORAGE

LINEAR
PREDICTIVE
DECODING

Fig. 6-17. The LPC mechanism.

frames from the speech analysis system give us information on
the pitch of the voice, the formant frequency characteristics,
and amplitude and voicing data. This array of information output by the digital speech processor is quite impressive but
necessary for eventual LPC encoding. The block labeled
"LINEAR PREDICTIVE ENCODING" in Fig. 6-17 resides within
the speech processing computer with rules for converting the
spectral content of speech to LPC parameters. The basic concept behind the linear predictive coding technique is that up-
coming speech samples can be estimated as a linear combination of past speech samples. So, in effect, the encoding block
becomes a short term forecaster or fortune teller of the speech
waveform. It outputs control parameters and numerical
coefficients which are used for the linear predictive regeneration of speech.

The control parameters which are produced by the linear predictive encoding process typically consist of amplitude and pitch information with a voiced/unvoiced speech decision control. The most significant data output by the LPC encoding process are the predictor coefficients which will ultimately be used by the digital filter speech reconstruction process. The number of these coefficients varies depending on the sampling rates and desired quality of reproduced speech, but in current market products the number of predictors is typically 10 to 12.

The output data from the linear predictive encoder is the digital information which is supplied to you in Read Only Memory (ROM) by the manufacturers for regenerating speech from your LPC synthesis system. Later in this section we will take a look at a typical LPC data frame and the effect of the various coefficients. Once the LPC data is stored in ROM in the synthesizer, the system may be commanded to speak through the linear predictive decoding process. This action occurs in the blocks at the right of Fig. 6-17. These blocks have been implemented into a single integrated circuit by several manufacturers to produce synthetic LPC speech with a minimum of electronic circuitry. A block diagram of one type of LPC synthesis integrated circuit from Texas Instruments (the first manufacturer to successfully implement LPC speech on a chip) is shown in Fig. 6-18.

This synthesizer block diagram which represents the internal workings of the Texas Instruments TMC-0281 (TMS5100) shows the flow of a complete LPC artificial speech reconstruction system. The logical flow of data in this figure is from the upper right to the left, then down through the dashed line, and out the lower right in the form of analog speech information. Circuitry above the dashed lines corresponds to digital processing of data to drive the LPC synthesis mechanism. Below the line are the circuit components which directly synthesize speech from the calculated LPC coefficients.

The individual blocks shown in this figure are not universal to all LPC synthesizers; this is just one particular implementation of the process as designed by the speech products group at Texas Instruments. However, the blocks in the lower portion of Fig. 6-18 represent fairly universal blocks needed for almost any type of LPC speech synthesis. These correspond to a pitch generator (remember the glottal pulse), a pseudo-random noise generator for fricative sounds, and a digital filtering system to

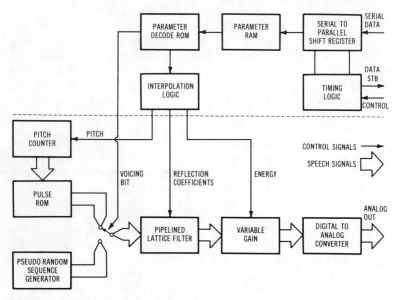

Fig. 6-18. LPC synthesizer block diagram.

modify the voiced and unvoiced sounds into speech. The final block within the LPC speech generating system is a digital-to-analog converter which converts the speech data from ones and zeros to a loudspeaker driving analog waveform.

The LPC synthesizer, like the analog formant synthesizer, is driven periodically with an updating frame rate fast enough to follow the dynamics of the human vocal tract. Depending on the integrated circuit manufacturer and number of reflection (predictor) coefficients used, typical frame rates vary from 40 to 100 times per second. In other words, every 10 to 25 milliseconds a complete new set of speech data is applied to the LPC synthesis circuitry to generate speech during the remainder of the frame period. If we take a closer look at a frame of LPC data and how it might relate to Fig. 6-18, then we can begin to get a better feel for the complexity of LPC synthesis. Fig. 6-19 is a visual description of LPC data is utilized in the Texas Instruments LPC technique. In this figure, the voiced data frame is represented at the top of the figure. Each block represents a piece of information needed by the LPC synthesizer to create a spoken output. The first block labeled EN-ERGY continuously controls the amplitude of the speech being

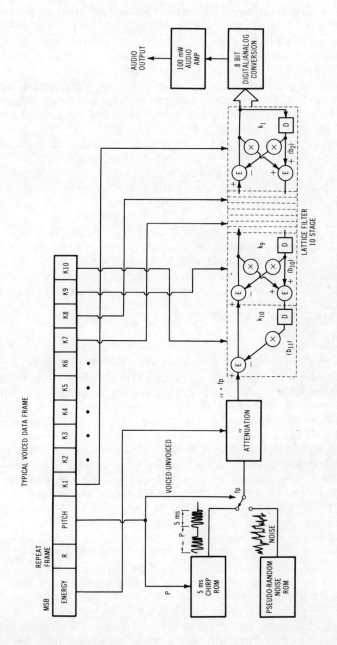

Fig. 6-19. A visual description of the Texas Instruments LPC data frame.

115

spoken. The next block, signifying a REPEAT FRAME, takes advantage of the slowly varying vocal tract characteristics for continuant sounds. For example, if the sound "ah" is to be spoken during an utterance for longer than one frame, then the repeat frame bit commands the synthesizer to repeat the previous ten filter coefficients (K1-K10). The addition of this repeat bit to the LPC frame data drops the number of blocks by almost 80% for repeated continuant sound data. The next block within the LPC frame is the PITCH control word which controls not only the pitch (or period P) of the glottal pulse synthesizer, it also controls the decision for voiced or unvoiced speech. If the pitch of a spoken utterance is zero, then by definition, the voiced-unvoiced switch selects the pseudo-random noise as an unvoiced input to the digital lattice filter.

The last ten blocks of the LPC data frame correspond to the predictor coefficients to be used by the digital lattice filter in regenerating the original speech. Each of these ten coefficients is a numerical value which sets a specific feedback gain within the lattice filter. Although this number of coefficients is not always used for speech (the number drops for unvoiced speech), this is the maximum length of the LPC data frame as devised by Texas Instruments.

The various types of data frames used within LPC speech synthesis tend to compact speech storage requirements and further reduce the ultimate digital data rate for speech. Within the TI-type synthesizers, there are five basic frame formats of digital speech information as shown in Fig. 6-20. Specifically, for the TMS5100, there are a maximum number of 49 bits of data for a full *voiced* frame. This particular frame format is used to create any speech characterized by a vibrating vocal cord. The fricative and stop consonants are generated by the *unvoiced* frame with the pitch control word set to zero. Notice that the number of filtering coefficients drops to four because the hissing sounds are generated further up in the vocal tract and, therefore, receive less vocal tract filtering. The data frame length of unvoiced speech is 28 bits which produces very efficient synthesis of speech considering the high frequency sounds generated. The next frame format in Fig. 6-20 is the *repeat* frame. As mentioned earlier, this frame is used to repeat any of the above frames while holding all of the coefficients K1-K10 constant. The drop in control frame length to 10 bits produces tremendous efficiency for sustained continuant type sounds. The last two frames within Fig. 6-20 are the *zero en-*

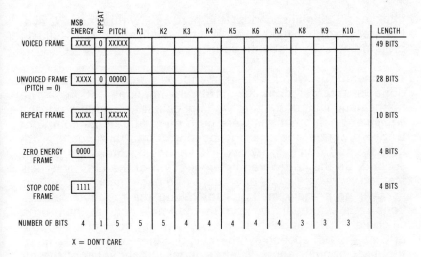

	MSB ENERGY	REPEAT	PITCH	K1	K2	K3	K4	K5	K6	K7	K8	K9	K10	LENGTH
VOICED FRAME	XXXX	0	XXXXX											49 BITS
UNVOICED FRAME (PITCH = 0)	XXXX	0	00000											28 BITS
REPEAT FRAME	XXXX	1	XXXXX											10 BITS
ZERO ENERGY FRAME	0000													4 BITS
STOP CODE FRAME	1111													4 BITS
NUMBER OF BITS	4	1	5	5	5	4	4	4	4	4	3	3	3	

X = DON'T CARE

Fig. 6-20. LPC data formats used by Texas Instruments.

ergy frame and the stop code frame. The zero energy frame is nothing more than spoken silence. This, in effect, turns the output of the synthesizer off to recreate pauses in the human speech output. The final stop frame format commands the synthesizer to stop speaking and return its attention to the controlling computer. Although the previously described specific types of data frames are used within the TI synthesis system, they are representative of those used by other manufacturers such as the General Instrument LPC synthesis system, the PARCOR systems from Japan, and the Telesensory LPC Systems.

The description of the linear predictive coding speech synthesis method must necessarily be limited to a hardware-type of description in this section because its basis is purely mathematical. If the linear predictive speech process was explained from the ground up, at least 10 to 20 pages of this book would contain nothing but equations. For those of you who would like to see these equations, they can be found within the books listed in the referenced reading material on LPC speech.

The process that occurs within the LPC synthesizer during speech output would be hard to simulate with any existing home computer. During speech, each of the predictor coefficients used by the digital filter is updated at a frame rate of approximately 50 times per second. For each updating of the filter (every 20 milliseconds), the hardware within the LPC synthesizer performs 4000 10 × 14 bit multiplications and 4000 14 bit additions. Try that with your home computer!

The means by which this tremendously fast computation is done is a rather complex hardware implementation of the mathematical algorithms for multiplication and addition. If the *equivalent* computations were performed in a home computer BASIC program, the speech updating frame rate would probably be one frame every 5 or 10 minutes rather than 50 per second. So the hardware implementation of the LPC synthesis method is the key to its operation! And each manufacturer has its own proprietary methods for taking the required calculations of linear predictive coding and implementing them on a silicon chip. No matter how this is eventually accomplished, the LPC method of speech synthesis is destined to become one of the most popular and efficient synthesis techniques of the future. It is a relative newcomer to the field of available speech synthesis products and is quickly gaining acceptance in the market place. Linear predictive coding speech is very close in sound to normal human speech while requiring a relatively low data rate. The cost of this technique is also relatively low because of its ease of silicon implementation. This results in a lower cost synthesizer to you.

Of course, one problem still exists (as with waveform encoded speech) in that you must rely on prerecorded vocabularies for your computer speech output. To alleviate this problem, several innovative manufacturers have produced phonetic and allophonic sounds in direct LPC code, and supplied these with the synthesizer chips. This capability within the LPC mechanism gives the user an unlimited vocabulary by phonetic concatenation of LPC speech sounds. These systems are very similar in operation to the phoneme formant-driven synthesizers described in the previous section. The coupling of the LPC technique with phoneme synthesis provides a tremendously powerful synthesis system for the user. However, the speech from this system sounds rather robotic because of the phoneme stringing, but is no worse than the sound of any phoneme-driven synthesizer. The compromise, of course, must be made in the user's requirements for an unlimited vocabulary with robotic sounding speech or human sounding speech with a manufacturer provided *canned* vocabulary. Of course, you may, if you have money to burn, go directly to the LPC integrated circuit manufacturers and request that they encode your own custom vocabulary into LPC speech. This is often done by the larger corporations which eventually produce millions of synthesis products with the same vocabulary and can "write off" the cost of the vocabulary encoding. To the home computer enthusiast, the encoding cost of $20 to $200 per word becomes rather prohibitive.

In the near future, LPC *encoding* devices should begin to appear on the market in limited quantities. As their production efficiency improves, the cost of these devices will drop and will allow the home computer enthusiast to generate his own vocabularies from his own voice. At that time, linear predictive coded speech should truly be the most efficient and least costly method of speech synthesis available.

Fringe Techniques

Although the currently existing speech synthesis methods are primarily limited to the three previously described techniques, others may appear in the future. These tomorrow-systems which are on the fringe of the technology are still in the laboratories. Most of these futuristic speech synthesizers are based on the mathematical simulation of the human vocal tract. In appearance they are very similar to LPC speech but with differences in the calculations for producing the voice output. Possibilities exist for speech synthesis using direct Fourier synthesis, Walsh function synthesis, and signal correlation and autocorrelation techniques referred to as PARCOR methods.

Most of these techniques are very similar in theory to LPC speech. Their differences lie in their hardware implementations. If any of these techniques eventually surpass the efficiency of LPC speech, it will be because their hardware implementation is less complicated. Only time will tell which speech synthesis system will be the system of the future. Considering the increase in complexity from each of the previous speech synthesis methods to the next, the next generation of speech synthesizers may be unrecognizable to us and today's technology.

chapter 7

Off-the-Shelf Speech Synthesis Systems

Assuming that you have read and understood the previous chapters in this book, the author would now venture to say that you have become an expert in the field of synthetic speech generation and its technology. One of the first uses for our new-found knowledge will be to examine the speech synthesizer products currently available to the computer enthusiast in today's market. The list of products is obviously not complete because new speech product related corporations are being formed almost daily. The eventual outcome of the current battle for the most popular speech synthesis will probably look much like the results of the earlier battle for the most popular microprocessors. Remember in the early days of the microprocessor there were a large number of products on the market with a variety of microcomputers from each of these products. As the larger and more powerful companies entered the market with their products, the smaller ones either grew to meet the competition or vanished. The same upheaval of the industry will most likely occur within the speech products market. For this reason, some of the products listed within this book may not be available. On the other hand, there will certainly be replacements to fill the void as each of the least-capitalized corporations drop out. The possibility also exists that the most efficient and best sounding speech synthesis system will gain its victory through public acceptance.

The following review of available synthetic speech products is based primarily on the data received from the manufacturers. If you see a system with a relatively brief review, then these manufacturers were either not interested in giving information (because of proprietary techniques) or they simply had very little product information available at the time of publication. The products will be reviewed in order of their speech synthesis technique used for generating speech. The first group of synthesizers will be of the waveform encoded/reconstructed type of speech synthesis. The next group of synthesis products will be based on the technology of analog formant synthesis. These are most often known as the phoneme synthesizers that allow unlimited vocabulary speech. The last, but not least, of the products to be reviewed operate with the Linear Predictive Coding (LPC) type of speech synthesis mechanism.

In some cases, the products will be reviewed as single integrated circuit chips because these may be purchased outright and integrated into your own computer system with your own design. If you are not so handy with hardware and are more interested in the end result, then the available speaking peripherals may better suit your taste. No matter which synthesizer you have or aspire to have, the manufacturers of each product should be cooperative in furnishing further information at your request.

Waveform Encoded/Reconstructed Systems

The first group of these commercial talkers that we will examine utilizes the digital recording and playback technique known as waveform encoding and reconstruction as described in the previous chapter. Some of the systems mentioned here are intended to be used on existing home computers such as the Apple®*, TRS-80®†, etc. Others are designed as self-standing units or meant to be used as computer peripherals with existing computers. The effect of each system is the same. Of course, the quality of speech for each system will typically depend upon the money that you invest to produce that resultant speech output.

A comparative table of the waveform encoded/reconstructed speech synthesizers to be reviewed in this section is given in

---

*Apple is a registered trademark of Apple Computer Corp.
†TRS-80 is a registered trademark of Radio Shack Div., Tandy Corp.

Table 7-1. The synthesizers listed in this table were available at the time of printing and the specifications and price of each system should be correct. The various synthesizers, listed in the lefthand column in this table, are described across the table with: (1) the types of synthesis, (2) the approximate size of the system, (3) the type of speech capability from the system, (4) the computer type with which the synthesizer may be used, and (5) the cost of a typical synthesis system.

CENTIGRAM CORP. "LISA"

The Centigram LISA system is a stand-alone computer peripheral terminal designed to be used transparently between a user teletype or CRT terminal and a host computer. This system is obviously one of the more expensive types available in the waveform encoded category (if that's what the parametric waveform encoding utilized by the Centigram Corporation might be considered to be). Since the technique is highly proprietary and very little information is available, it defaults into this category for our consideration. A diagram of how the LISA voice output terminal might be connected to a typical computer system is given in Fig. 7-1. One of the features of this system is that it can be connected between a keyboard and computer as a transparent peripheral for generating speech from existing systems.

The speech terminal shown in Fig. 7-2 is the LISA voice output device. It is normally connected on-line between the computer and its keyboard/display user terminal. During operation, the

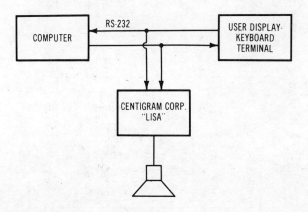

Fig. 7-1. The LISA speech synthesizer.

Table 7-1. A Review of Commercial Synthesizers as of 1982 (Direct Waveform Coded/Reconstructed)

Company	Synthesis Type	Size	Speech Capability	Computer Type	Cost
Centigram "LISA"	Parametric Waveform Coding	12.5×11.4×4.2 in (31.7×29× 10.6 cm)	Prestored Vocabulary	Any RS-232 SERIAL	
CHEAPTALK (TRS-80)	Fm Waveform Coding/ Playback	Software Only	Stored Users Vocabulary	TRS-80, H-8	$20.00
Computalker Consultants "CompuCorder"	Direct Waveform Coding	5×10 in (12.7×25.4 cm) PC. Card	Stored Users Vocabulary	S-100, IEEE-696	$300
Micromint "Micromouth"	National "DIGITALKER" Chip (see below)	7×3×2-in (17.7×7.6×5 cm)	ROM Purchased Vocabulary	APPLE, TRS-80, S-100, H-8	$150
National Semiconductor "DIGITALKER"	APDCM-Waveform Coding	Various	ROM Purchased Vocabulary	Stand Alone Boards and Chips; Any	$40 to $200
Telesensory Speech Systems "SERIES III"	CRC Waveform Coding	4×4½-in (10.1×11.4 cm) Board	ROM Purchased Vocabulary	Any Parallel TTL Port	$350
Voicetek "Cognivox VIO"	Direct Waveform Coding	5×6×1.25 in (12.7×15.2×3.2 cm)	User-Spoken *With* Recognition	APPLE, TRS-80, PET, AIM-65	$150 to $250

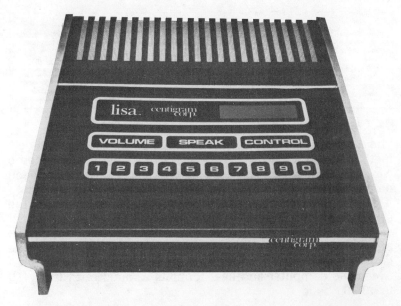

Fig. 7-2. The LISA voice output terminal. *(Courtesy Centigram Corp.)*

speaking peripheral captures its own speech commands and speech data while allowing the passage of normal computer commands between the keyboard and computer. The vocabulary of the LISA system utilizes the storage of words, sentences, or any length of speech on the host computer disk for playback during spoken utterances. By operating in this manner, the LISA system provides unlimited vocabulary speech for the computer to which it's connected.

The "canned" vocabulary for disk storage is provided by the Centigram Corporation as a disk file. Then during execution it is transferred from the computer to the LISA by the application program. Finally, LISA is commanded to speak words from the vocabulary by the user operating program. The vocabulary on the disk file may come from either a prepared script that you provide to Centigram with a fee for vocabulary encoding, or from your own voice libraries made with the Centigram voice library generator. The capabilities of this rather expensive device allow you to make your own vocabularies with the ease of a digital tape recording. The actual flow of data within the computer to the LISA talker is shown in Fig. 7-3. The simplicity of this interface allows the speech system to be connected to almost any type of host computer that needs a voice output peripheral.

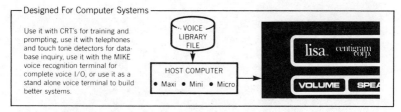

Fig. 7-3. Using the LISA system. *(Courtesy Centigram Corp.)*

The LISA speech output system operates with a synthesis method referred to by the Centigram Corporation as parametric waveform synthesis. This type of synthesis requires a speech data rate of approximately 300 to 600 bytes per second, placing it in the efficiency range of LPC synthesized speech. In fact, the synthesis methods seem to have a great deal of similarity, but since the Centigram parametric waveform encoding method is proprietary, very little information is available. However, it is known that the system operates on RS-232 data flowing between the computer and user terminal at baud rates from 110 to 19,200 baud.

Internal to the LISA synthesizer peripheral is a Z80 microprocessor with 16K of random access memory (RAM) to store the spoken outputs. The audio from the system is available at a 2-watt power level from a four-inch speaker allowing more than room-filling sound. A rather considerate feature added to the LISA is a standard earphone connector. This allows the computer user the privacy of the spoken output and prevents annoying others with spoken computer messages. Not only does the Centigram Corporation have this system available for speech processing, it also provides the MIKE speech recognition system and several other systems for computer-to-user speech interaction.

CHEAPTALK BY GREGORY ALAN SAVILLE

This is one of the few pure software speech systems available for home computers which requires almost no additional hardware. The simplicity of the Cheaptalk speech synthesizer is due to its waveform encoding process. It is designed primarily to operate with the Radio Shack TRS-80 series computers and the Heath H-8 computers. A single bit input/output port is all that is required to digitize spoken words and reproduce them. An inexpensive audio amplifier and microphone can be used to digitize and reproduce the speech waveform. In either of the applicable computers, a simple hardware modification is required for speech waveform *encoding*. In the case of the Heath H-8 computer, a single jumper wire is required for waveform encoding. Reproduction of the encoded speech requires a change of one integrated circuit pin on the front panel board to the H-8 internal speaker for speech playback. The Radio Shack TRS-80, on the other hand, will playback waveform encoded speech to the cassette audio output with no modifications. Speech waveform *encoding* in the TRS-80 computer requires a slight modification internal to the keyboard (or the addition of a few external gates) to provide waveform signal gating. The software version of the Cheaptalk system will digitize (waveform encoded) your *own* voice when applied to the appropriate input port, and then play back your speech upon command to the audio output system.

The speech encoding process utilized by the Cheaptalk system is one not described in the previous chapter on waveform encoding. It is, however, somewhat similar to the delta modulation encoding process in that it stores only a single bit of data for each sample. The same process is used by several other software-only speech synthesizers and is referred to as the frequency modulation (fm) method of waveform encoding. An illustration of this process is shown in Fig. 7-4. The speech input waveform at the top of the figure is sampled approximately 4000 times per second to see if the amplitude of the signal is above or below the preset threshold. Since the threshold inputs are simple TTL gates, the threshold levels are 0.8 volt for a logic 0 and 2.4 volts for a logic 1. As the input speech varies in amplitude between these two thresholds, the digital encoding of the speech varies from a 0 to a 1. The output pulse stream at the bottom of Fig. 7-4 represents both the single bit data stored in memory and the data output to the speaker for speech playback. Obviously there is little resemblance between two waveforms but the somewhat distorted output speech is still recognizable. Considering the inexpensive cost of the system, it is an excellent way to generate the first words from your computer.

The Cheaptalk system is available on cassette tape for the TRS-80 computer and on an H17 disk for the Heath H-8 computer. The software supplied provides both the speech encoding and playback capabilities for either computer. Both computer programs contain a demonstration or talking program to help your computer speak. These have words spoken by Mr. Saville

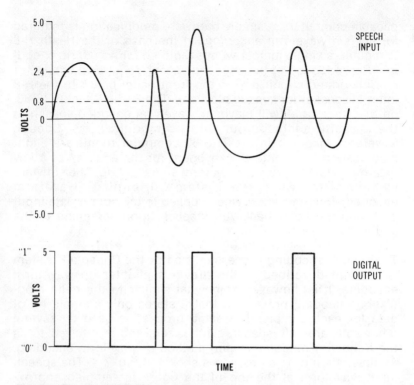

Fig. 7-4. The single-bit FM encoding process.

which provide vocal hex memory dumps and a demonstration alphabetic sequence.

COMPUTALKER CONSULTANTS "COMPUCORDER"

The Computalker Consultants "CompuCorder" is a versatile low-cost digital storage and output device. The speech board, which is essentially a solid-state tape recorder, is the second major product from a speech synthesis company whose origin dates back almost to the beginning of the microprocessor. Accordingly, this company delivered its first home computer speech synthesizer in November 1976. The original synthesizer known as the CT-1 was designed for the S-100 bus, and utilized the analog formant synthesis method of speech synthesis.

The CT-1 synthesizer, which has historical significance because of its early introduction to the home computer market, is shown in Fig. 7-5. Its design was quite advanced for its time. If

128

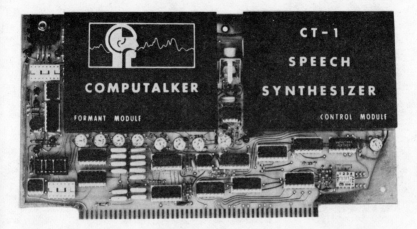

Fig. 7-5. The historic Computalker Consultants COMPUTALKER CT-1.
(Courtesy Computalker Consultants)

it were still on the market today it would be thoroughly described in the next section on formant synthesizers. However,
its rather high cost of approximately $600, including software,
made it quite a luxury item for the average home computer
hobbyist. It has since been dropped from production by Computalker Consultants and replaced with the direct waveform
encoding/reconstruction synthesizer: The CompuCorder. The
CompuCorder, unlike the original CT-1 synthesizer, is available
today as a home computer peripheral.

The Computalker Consultants CompuCorder shown in Fig. 7-6
produces high quality speech in any language, speaking with
any voice, male or female. The digital recorder also has the
capability of storing and replaying music and sound effects.
The CompuCorder's vocabulary is generated by the user by
simply speaking into the user furnished microphone. The spoken vocabulary is then digitized using a hardware data-
compression technique on the CompuCorder circuit board. The
resulting compacted speech data is stored in the computer's
memory and replayed on command under software control.
The user must also furnish an audio amplifier and loudspeaker
to provide the correct volume for normal room listening levels.

The CompuCorder provides you with the ability to select a
compromise between the output speech quality and the speech
storage memory requirements. User selectable rates are 1.25K,
2K, 3K, and 4K bytes per second of speech. Depending on the

129

Fig. 7-6. The current CompuCorder speech synthesizer. *(Courtesy Computalker Consultants)*

memory availability in your computer you may choose the appropriate speech rate. At the 4K byte per second rate, the speech output approaches that of a true tape recording. This is an effective sampling rate of 32,000 bits per second! A 64K byte computer can store approximately 16 seconds of speech at this rate and produce completely normal sounding, crystal-clear speech output. If the computer is combined with a floppy disk for speech storage, the duration of the speech output will increase accordingly. The software that is available for the CompuCorder is written in 8080 assembler code and supplied on CP/M®* disk. Other disk formats are available on request at extra charge. This synthesizer is ideal for the user who wishes to create a vocabulary from his own voice at a reasonably low cost.

MICROMOUTH™

The Micromouth speech synthesizer interface is produced by Micromint, Inc. using a design proposed by Steve Ciarcia in the June 1981 issue of *Byte Magazine*. The synthesizer utilizes the National Semiconductor Digitalker chip set to produce delta modulated synthetic speech. The synthesis system is sold either in kit form, or assembled and tested for a price ranging from $120 to approximately $200. Although the specific computers supported include the Apple II and the TRS-80, it may also be interfaced to other computers using parallel data ports.

---

*CP/M is a registered trademark of Digital Research Inc.

The Micromouth® speech synthesizer board is shown in Fig. 7-7. The single board version is a direct plug-in peripheral to the Apple II computer. A cabinet version of the same unit is supplied as an interface for the TRS-80 computer. It includes the interface ribbon cable for connecting to the expansion bus connector of either the Model I or Model III TRS-80. The vocabulary included with the Micromouth speech synthesizer consists of two 64K bit ROMs which contain the vocabulary shown in Table 7-2. The words within this vocabulary are also supplied by National Semiconductor on two prestored vocabulary ROMs.

Fig. 7-7. The Micromouth speech synthesizer. *(Courtesy Micromint Inc.)*

The method used by the computers to access words within the speech synthesizer consists of either a *poke* or *out* statement. As the output code for each individual vocabulary word is supplied to the Micromouth, a *busy* signal line informs the computer that the system is still speaking. At the end of the speech period, the synthesizer signals the computer that it is ready for the next 8-bit binary vocabulary address byte. Because of this operation, the overhead required to create a speaking program is very low. For instance, to say "At the mark, the time is 2:45 PM . . . (beep)," only about 15 accesses of the synthesizer are required. Each access corresponds to a particular word, number, or space so the computer has considerable time during the speech to perform other operations. The Micromouth is a very simple and efficient speech synthesizer. The installation of the Micromouth into either the TRS-80 or Apple II computers is shown in Figs. 7-8 and 7-9.

Table 7-2. Digitalker™ Vocabulary.

Word	8-Bit Binary Address SW8 SW1		8-Bit Binary Address SW8 SW1		8-Bit Binary Address SW8 SW1
THIS IS DIGITALKER	00000000	Q	00110000	IS	01100000
ONE	00000001	R	00110001	IT	01100001
TWO	00000010	S	00110010	KILO	01100010
THREE	00000011	T	00110011	LEFT	01100011
FOUR	00000100	U	W0110100	LESS	01100100
FIVE	00000101	V	00110101	LESSER	01100101
SIX	00000110	W	00110110	LIMIT	01100110
SEVEN	00000111	X	00110111	LOW	01100111
EIGHT	00001000	Y	00111000	LOWER	01101000
NINE	00001001	Z	00111001	MARK	01101001
TEN	00001010	AGAIN	00111010	METER	01101010
ELEVEN	00001011	AMPERE	00111011	MILE	01101011
TWELVE	00001100	AND	00111100	MILLI	01101100
THIRTEEN	00001101	AT	00111101	MINUS	01101101
FOURTEEN	00001110	CANCEL	00111110	MINUTE	01101110
FIFTEEN	00001111	CASE	00111111	NEAR	01101111
SIXTEEN	00010000	CENT	01000000	NUMBER	01110000
SEVENTEEN	00010001	400HERTZ TONE	01000001	OF	01110001
EIGHTEEN	00010010	80HERTZ TONE	01000010	OFF	01110010
NINETEEN	00010011	20MS SILENCE	01000011	ON	01110011
TWENTY	00010100	40MS SILENCE	01000100	OUT	01110100
THIRTY	00010101	80MS SILENCE	01000101	OVER	01110101
FORTY	00010110	160MS SILENCE	01000110	PARENTHESIS	01110110
FIFTY	00010111	320MS SILENCE	01000111	PERCENT	01110111
SIXTY	00011000	CENTI	01001000	PLEASE	01111000
SEVENTY	00011001	CHECK	01001001	PLUS	01111001
EIGHTY	00011010	COMMA	01001010	POINT	01111010

Word	8-Bit Binary Address SW8 SW1	Word	8-Bit Binary Address SW8 SW1	Word	8-Bit Binary Address SW8 SW1
NINETY	00011011	CONTROL	01001011	POUND	01111011
HUNDRED	00011100	DANGER	01001100	PULSES	01111100
THOUSAND	00011101	DEGREE	01001101	RATE	01111101
MILLION	00011110	DOLLAR	01001110	RE	01111110
ZERO	00011111	DOWN	01001111	READY	01111111
A	00100000	EQUAL	01010000	RIGHT	10000000
B	00100001	ERROR	01010001	SS (Note 1)	10000001
C	00100010	FEET	01010010	SECOND	10000010
D	00100011	FLOW	01010011	SET	10000011
E	00100100	FUEL	01010100	SPACE	10000100
F	00100101	GALLON	01010101	SPEED	10000101
G	00100110	GO	01010110	STAR	10000110
H	00100111	GRAM	01010111	START	10000111
I	00101000	GREAT	01011000	STOP	10001000
J	00101001	GREATER	01011001	THAN	10001001
K	00101010	HAVE	01011010	THE	10001010
L	00101011	HIGH	01011011	TIME	10001011
M	00101100	HIGHER	01011100	TRY	10001100
N	00101101	HOUR	01011101	UP	10001101
O	00101110	IN	01011110	VOLT	10001110
P	00101111	INCHES	01011111	WEIGHT (Note 2)	10001111

Note 1: "SS" makes any singular word plural

Note 2: Address 143 is the last legal address in this particular word list. Exceeding address 143 will produce pieces of unintelligible speech data.

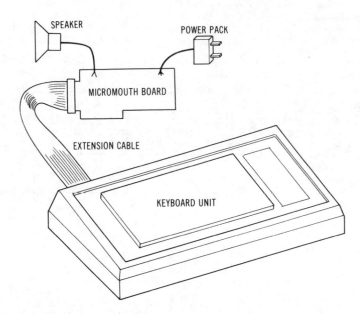

Fig. 7-8. The TRS-80® version of Micromouth. *(Courtesy Micromint Inc.)*

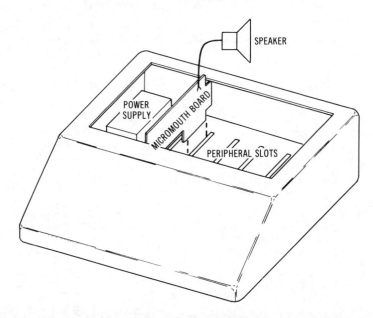

Fig. 7-9. The Apple II® version of Micromouth. *(Courtesy Micromint Inc.)*

NATIONAL SEMICONDUCTOR "DIGITALKER™"

The Digitalker speech synthesis system is available in several configurations. The heart of the National Semiconductor system is the MM54104 speech processor chip (SPC). This is a single 40-pin integrated circuit shown in Fig. 7-10. The circuitry within the MM54104 speech processor chip is shown in the block diagram of Fig. 7-11. The complexity of the Digitalker speech processor chip diagram illustrates the modifications that National Semiconductor has made to the standard delta modulation process. Although there is a block called "DEMOD" decoder, the actual delta demodulation functions are overshadowed by support registers and amplifiers. These peripheral registers provide a further reduction in the required effective speech data rate, therefore reducing the speech storage requirements. The SPC terminals marked SW1 through SW8

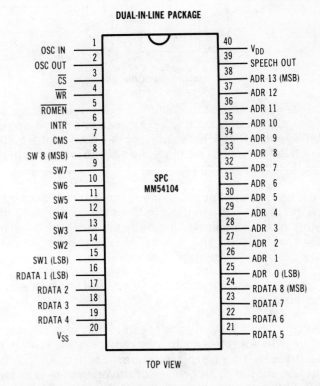

Fig. 7-10. Pinouts of DIGITALKER™ speech processor chip (MM54104).
(Courtesy National Semiconductor Corp.)

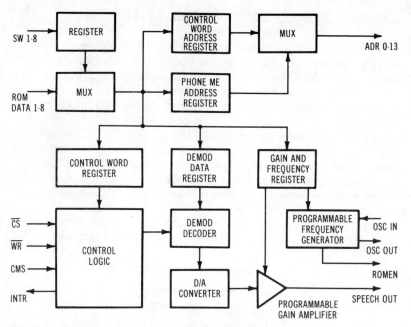

Fig. 7-11. The SPC MM54104 internal block diagram.

comprise an 8-bit start address input bus which allows up to 256 separately defined sounds or expressions to be accessed from the speech ROM. By supplying an 8-bit word to these ports and taking the WR line high, the speech word or phrase is accessed and speech begins.

The simplicity of a minimum Digitalker speech synthesis system is shown in Fig. 7-12. When used in this manner, the SPC needs no driving microprocessor. Instead, an array of nine input switches is used to set the spoken phrase and begin speech. The only peripheral components required in the minimum configuration are an audio amplifier and associated low-pass output filter, a speech vocabulary ROM, and the clock crystal oscillator circuit.

The Digitalker speech synthesizer system may also be easily interfaced to a microprocessor bus by replacing the switch input control lines with microprocessor controls. A typical configuration for the microprocessor driven system is shown in Fig. 7-13. The command lines to the SPC are very simple and easily understood. The data lines D0 through D7 provide the

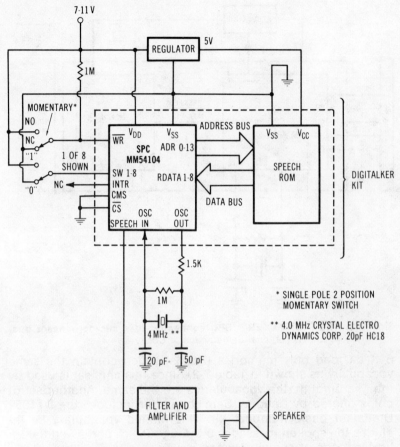

Fig. 7-12. The DIGITALKER™ speech synthesizer used with switch controls.
(Courtesy National Semiconductor Corp.)

start phrase or word address for speech output. The WR line is
equivalent to the read/write line (R/W) which strobes the correct data into the speech control register. The A0 is the command select line which controls the manner in which the SPC
services the interrupt (INTR) signal back to the microprocessor.
The chip select (CS) pin readies the SPC to receive commands
at a decoded microprocessor memory address.

In addition to providing the basic speech processor chip, National Semiconductor provides several vocabulary ROMs with
preencoded vocabularies to serve almost universal situations.
The DT1050 Digitalker standard vocabulary kit includes two

137

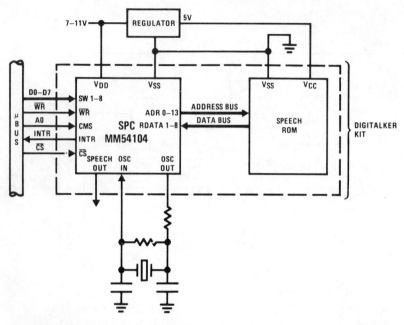

Fig. 7-13. The DIGITALKER™ SPC connected to a microprocessor bus.
(Courtesy National Semiconductor Corp.)

64K bit read only memories (ROMs) which contain the same vocabulary as shown in Table 7-2. Since this chip set is used by the Micromouth, the vocabularies are the same. Another set of chips offered by National Semiconductor includes the DT1052 Digitalker basic numbers kit. This limited vocabulary kit includes the spoken messages 0 through 9, ".", and five different time periods of spoken silence.

If the vocabularies within the previous ROMs are not adequate for your application, National Semiconductor also supplies the DT1057 Digitalker® speech ROMs with another standard vocabulary. The combination of this vocabulary with the previous ones will surely serve most of the needs that you might create. This "second" standard word kit is shown in Table 7-3. The words within this vocabulary tend to closely support the previously listed vocabulary words to provide a fairly comprehensive vocabulary for almost any application. To verify this, you might consider an application with a particular phrase; then see if you can find the words or substitutes that you need within the vocabulary lists of Table 7-2 and Table 7-3. Remember, that not only can you speak words with intervening pauses, but you also

138

can concatenate parts of words and phrases to form longer words. For instance, in Table 7-3, if you needed to speak *megohms* then you would supply in sequence the address 45 (hex), and 52 (hex) without an intervening pause.

If you would like to investigate the Digitalker speech synthesis system without all the complications of hardware connections, then National Semiconductor supplies a complete speech synthesis evaluation board shown in Fig. 7-14: the DT1000. This board contains the SPC, two read only memories with the vocabulary shown in Table 7-2, the low pass output filter and amplifier, and a small preprogrammed microprocessor. To use this speech evaluation board, only a single 5-volt to 11-volt power supply and inexpensive loudspeaker are required. The demonstration board shows the extreme flexibility and ease of application of the Digitalker chip set. The Digitalker system manufactured by National Semiconductor is one of the major speech synthesis chip systems available on today's market with direct waveform encoding/decoding of speech. Since the vocabularies needed to create speech from this system are encoded by the people at National Semiconductor, the capabilities for creating your own vocabulary are rather limited. Custom vocabularies can be encoded for you by National Semiconductor, but the cost per word is expensive. This system is best suited to those applications which use the preexisting canned vocabularies in limited cost applications.

TELESENSORY SPEECH SYSTEMS SERIES III

The Series III speech synthesizer module is one of a family of speech products offered by Telesensory Speech Systems. In Fig. 7-15, the Series III module is the medium-size printed circuit board at the lower right of the picture. The smaller board at the lower left is the Series II system which is being phased out of production and the large board is the LPC SPEECH 1000®️ synthesizer system to be described later in this chapter.

The Series III synthesizer module is a complete speech synthesizer circuit board designed for simple system integration. The synthesizer module contains Telesensory's proprietary speech synthesizer, a basic 119-word vocabulary, a speech low pass filter, and an audio amplifier. Also provided on the speech module is an extra ROM socket for adding custom vocabularies. The module operates with a single +5-volt power supply and can generate approximately 100 seconds of synthesized

Table 7-3. The Contents of the DT1057 Vocabulary ROMs.

Word	8-Bit Binary Address SW8 → SW1	Word	8-Bit Binary Address SW8 → SW1	Word	8-Bit Binary Address SW8 → SW1
ABORT	00000000	FARAD	00101100	PER	01011000
ADD	00000001	FAST	00101101	PICO	01011001
ADJUST	00000010	FASTER	00101110	PLACE	01011010
ALARM	00000011	FIFTH	00101111	PRESS	01011011
ALERT	00000100	FIRE	00110000	PRESSURE	01011100
ALL	00000101	FIRST	00110001	QUARTER	01011101
ASK	00000110	FLOOR	00110010	RANGE	01011110
ASSISTANCE	00000111	FORWARD	00110011	REACH	01011111
ATTENTION	00001000	FROM	00110100	RECEIVE	01100000
BRAKE	00001001	GAS	00110101	RECORD	01100001
BUTTON	00001010	GET	00110110	REPLACE	01100010
BUY	00001011	GOING	00110111	REVERSE	01100011
CALL	00001100	HALF	00111000	ROOM	01100100
CAUTION	00001101	HELLO	00111001	SAFE	01100101
CHANGE	00001110	HELP	00111010	SECURE	01100110
CIRCUIT	00001111	HERTZ	00111011	SELECT	01100111
CLEAR	00010000	HOLD	00111100	SEND	01101000
CLOSE	00010001	INCORRECT	00111101	SERVICE	01101001
COMPLETE	00010010	INCREASE	00111110	SIDE	01101010
CONNECT	00010011	INTRUDER	00111111	SLOW	01101011
CONTINUE	00010100	JUST	01000000	SLOWER	01101100
COPY	00010101	KEY	01000001	SMOKE	01101101
CORRECT	00010110	LEVEL	01000010	SOUTH	01101110
DATE	00010111	LOAD	01000011	STATION	01101111
DAY	00011000	LOCK	01000100	SWITCH	01110000
DECREASE	00011001	MEG	01000101	SYSTEM	01110001
DEPOSIT	00011010	MEGA	01000110	TEST	01110010
DIAL	00011011	MICRO	01000111	TH (NOTE 2)	01110011

Word	8-Bit Binary Address SW8 → SW1	Word	8-Bit Binary Address SW8 → SW1	Word	8-Bit Binary Address SW8 → SW1
DIVIDE	00011100	MORE	01001000	THANK	01110100
DOOR	00011101	MOVE	01001001	THIRD	01110101
EAST	00011110	NANO	01001010	THIS	01110110
ED (NOTE 1)	00011111	NEED	01001011	TOTAL	01110111
ED (NOTE 1)	00100000	NEXT	01001100	TURN	01111000
ED (NOTE 1)	00100001	NO	01001101	USE	01111001
ED (NOTE 1)	00100010	NORMAL	01001110	UTH (NOTE 3)	01111010
EMERGENCY	00100011	NORTH	01001111	WAITING	01111011
END	00100100	NOT	01010000	WARNING	01111100
ENTER	00100101	NOTICE	01010001	WATER	01111101
ENTRY	00100110	OHMS	01010010	WEST	01111110
ER	00100111	ONWARD	01010011	SWITCH	01111111
EVACUATE	00101000	OPEN	01010100	WINDOW	10000000
EXIT	00101001	OPERATOR	01010101	YES	10000001
FAIL	00101010	OR	01010110	ZONE	10000010
FAILURE	00101011	PASS	01010111		

Note 1: "ED" is a suffix that can be used to make any present tense word become a past tense word. The way we say "ED," however, does vary from one word to the next. For that reason, we have offered 4 different "ED" sounds. It is suggested that each "ED" be tested with the desired word for best quality results. Address 31 "ED" or 32 "ED" should be used with words ending in "T" or "D," such as exit or load. Address 34 "ED" should be used with words ending with soft sounds such as ask. Address 33 "ED" should be used with all other words.

Note 2: "TH" is a suffix that can be added to words like six, seven, eight to form adjective words like sixth, seventh, eighth.

Note 3: "UTH" is a suffix that can be added to words like twenty, thirty, forty to form adjective words like thirtieth, fortieth, etc.

Note 4: Address 130 is the last legal address in this particular word list. Exceeding address 130 will produce pieces of unintelligible invalid speech data.

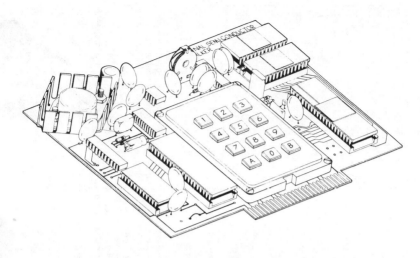

Fig. 7-14. The DT1000 DIGITALKER™ speech synthesizer system evaluation board. *(Courtesy National Semiconductor Corp.)*

Fig. 7-15. The Telesensory family of speech synthesizers.

human speech. Although the actual method of speech synthesis is not fully disclosed by Telesensory Speech Systems, it is referred to as Custom ROM Controller (CRC) speech and is most likely encoded with delta modulation. A block diagram of the Series III synthesizer module is shown in Fig. 7-16. Since the module is a self-contained system, it needs only a command word and strobe to create speech. A *busy* signal from the module indicates to the controlling external processor that the synthesizer is still talking. The system can be used with a simple switch interface (without a microprocessor) to create speech. This configuration, which can serve as a stand alone synthesizer, is shown in Fig. 7-17. Used in this manner, only nine total switches are required to select up to 256 possible utterances.

The Series III module may also be connected directly to a microprocessor parallel input/output port. This allows you to control the spoken utterances under program control. The connection of the Series III speech module to a typical microprocessor input/output port interface is shown in Fig. 7-18. This figure illustrates the simplicity of the connections required to create computer-controlled synthesized speech.

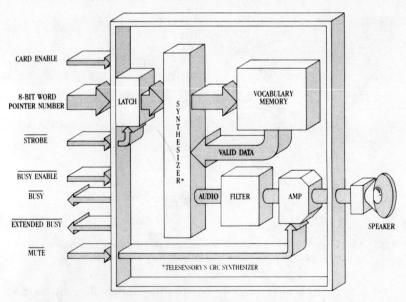

Fig. 7-16. The Telesensory Series III speech synthesizer block diagram.
(Courtesy Telesensory Speech Systems)

143

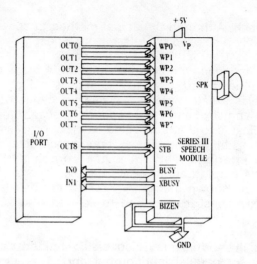

Fig. 7-17. The Telesensory Series III speech synthesizer with switch controls. *(Courtesy Telesensory Speech Systems).*

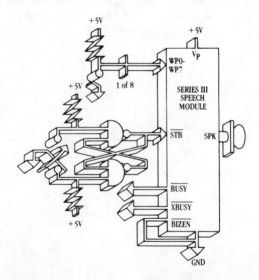

Fig. 7-18. A typical Series III microprocessor interface using a parallel input/output port. *(Courtesy Telesensory Speech Systems)*

The basic vocabulary word list for the Series III synthesizer module contains words which will serve most applications for status and numeric information transfer. The people at Telesensory Speech Systems provide a telephone number—not a toll-free one—for automatic speech demonstration of the Telesensory products. By dialing (415) 856-0225 and listening to the spoken messages, you can hear the sounds of the Telesensory family of speech synthesizers. This telephone demonstration is quite unique in that it is not a recording, but rather an actual computer generated demonstration; when you dial the number, you will be listening to a computer. This is evident as you progress into the demonstration because it is interactive. After the introductory synthetic speech message, you are presented with a verbal menu of codes that you can manually enter with a Touch-Tone dial. The following codes are given as the menu choices:

1	Repeat Menu
2 or 3	Text-to-Speech Synthesis Demonstration
4 or 5	Speech 1000 LPC Demonstration
6 or 7	Series III Module Demonstration

The demonstration number is quite unique in that it allows your interaction to determine what you hear. Since the number is computer controlled, it appears to be available almost 24 hours per day. Thus, you may place a call to the number during the low-rate hours.

VOICETEK "COGNIVOX"
The Cognivox speech synthesizer also serves as a speech recognition device. The VIO series of voice input/output peripherals is designed to interface to the major home computers of today. The computers supported are:

Cognivox Model	Computer Supported
VIO-1001	Rockwell AIM-65
VIO-1002	Commodore PET
VIO-1003	Apple II
VIO-132	Exidy Sorcerer
VIO-232	Z80 Based Systems
VIO-332	TRS-80 Level II 16K
VIO-432	Commodore PET

The VIO-1000 series of voice input/output peripherals offers excellent recognition performance and high quality voice output for the above listed computers. The remainder of the VIO peripherals provide a more economical voice input/output capabilities with a slight decrease in the fidelity of the speech output.

The capabilities of the VIO-1000 series peripherals include the recognition of up to 32 words or short phrases, and a similar capability for speech synthesis. Voice generation is created by direct digital recording of the user's voice. This form of waveform encoding allows you to create your own custom vocabulary. The synthesis systems generally are supplied in a quality injection molded case with a built-in audio amplifier and three-inch loudspeaker. Also supplied are the input microphone, power supply, program cassette, and user manual. This system is a rather inexpensive method of getting your feet wet in voice synthesis *and* recognition technology. More information can be obtained on the desired computer peripherals by writing directly to Voicetek.

Analog Formant Speech Synthesizers

The next group of speech synthesizers to be discussed talk by formant frequency synthesis of human speech. The sounds of these synthesizers are typically robotic in nature because they do not rely on direct reproduction of speech for their output. However, the capability for an unlimited vocabulary very often overshadows the disadvantages of the unnatural sounding speech. In particular, if a limited number of listeners can be trained to understand the phonetic formant speech, then these types of synthesizers are perfectly acceptable and interchangeable with the other speech technologies.

While this technique for generating speech synthesis has been around for quite some time, it is still a strong contender in today's speech market. The list of available formant synthesis speech synthesizers is shown in Table 7-4. The capabilities of each of these synthesizers are quite powerful owing to the phoneme type synthesis that they employ. Now, let's examine these analog simulations of the human vocal tract.

KURZWEIL COMPUTER PRODUCTS READING MACHINE

Although the Kurzweil Reading Machine (KRM) is not primarily a direct computer peripheral or for that matter designed to be one, it is a significant development in speech synthesis. The KRM is a direct optical reader/speech synthesizer interface designed primarily to aid the handicapped in reading.

Table 7-4. Currently Available Analog Formant Synthesizers.

Company	Synthesis Type	Size	Speech Capability	Computer Type	Cost
Kurzweil Reading Machine KRM	Phoneme Formants	Table Top	Spoken Text From Optical Reader	RS-232 SERIAL Port	$30,000
Micromint "Sweet Talker"	Votrax® SC-0lA Chip	3×4-in (7.6×10.2 cm) P.C. Card	Unlimited-Phoneme	APPLE II, PARALLEL TTL	About $150
Votrax SC-01A	Phoneme Formant	22-pin DIP	Unlimited-Phoneme	Any	About $70.00
Votrax Type 'N Talk	Phoneme Formant	8×5×3 in (20.3×12.7×7.6 cm)	Text-to-Speech	RS-232 SERIAL Port	$375

The Kurzweil reading machine provides personal direct access to printed and typewritten information for unsighted and visually impaired individuals. The system referred to as the KRM Model III provides in a relatively compact size a reading system which operates very similarly to a standard office copier. The reading system utilizes phonetic synthesis of speech derived from an optical character recognition system to provide unlimited speech capability directly from printed text. An example of the use of the KRM Model III is shown in Fig. 7-19. When used in this manner, with a book placed face down over the reading scanner, the system optically tracks and decodes printed text to verbally read the contents of the book. A small control console provides a convenient control panel which enables the user to temporarily halt the machine, back up to hear one or more lines over again, skip forward in the text, locate a particular word and have that word spelled out, or simply control the page reading format capabilities. Also included on the small control panel are adjustments for volume, speech rate, and pitch. The 10-inch x 9-inch x 2-inch control unit has an internal loudspeaker from which the phonetically converted text is spoken.

Fig. 7-19. The Kurzweil Reading Machine Model III in use. (*Courtesy Kurzweil Computer Products*)

The complete electronics of the Kurzweil reading machine are shown in Fig. 7-20. In addition to the control panel at the lower left of the photo, the optical tracking system sits atop the electronic control unit of the optical scanning system. The optical tracking system utilizes a linear scanning array camera to automatically read documents up to 11 inches x 14 inches in size. The electronic control unit for the tracking system contains the circuitry necessary to perform scanning, character recognition, and conversion of the text to phoneme functions for speech output. In order to make the reading system more flexible, Kurzweil has placed a digital cassette drive on the front panel of the electronic control unit for loading software programs needed to operate the reading machine. This allows flexibility for changes and options in the reading system's operation.

Fig. 7-20. The KRM Model III electronics package. *(Courtesy Kurzweil Computer Products)*

To illustrate the complexity of the reading process that the KRM performs, the people at Kurzweil Computer Products have prepared a reading flowchart which tracks the machine's operation. The sequence of events that occurs during reading is shown in Fig. 7-21 not only to illustrate the machine's operation, but also to give you an insight into how complex speech synthesis applications may be. In this diagram, the text or printed matter is optically scanned by the character recognition camera and converted through image enhancement to elec-

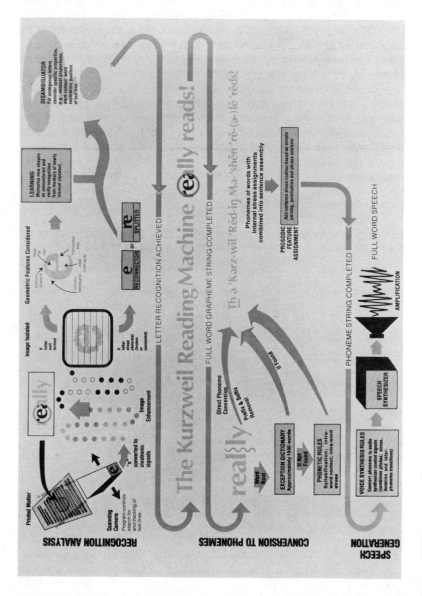

Fig. 7-21. The internal operation of the KRM Model III. *(Courtesy Kurzweil Computer Products)*

tronic signals. The resultant electronic signals are then processed through a rather complex pattern recognition program to determine the identification of each individual letter. This process is easily as complicated as the speech generation process. After the printed text has been converted to electronic text "strings," the system must then convert the deciphered material into phonemes for driving the speech synthesizer. The illustrations of the dictionary capabilities and phonetic rule conversions used are rather typical of most text-to-speech synthesizers. The output from the system is phonetically spoken text which requires some skill in understanding, but provides a reading capability where none existed before. This machine is obviously a very humanitarian application of speech synthesis. Its ultimate application is far removed from the talking vending machine.

MICROMINT "SWEET TALKER"

The Sweet Talker is a second speech synthesis peripheral marketed by Micromint, Inc. Whereas the previous "Micromouth" utilizes the Digitalker chip set for its speech output, the Sweet Talker relies on the Votrax®* SC-01A phonetic speech synthesizer chip. The Sweet Talker is a single, small printed circuit board available in two formats. The Apple II version plugs directly into the peripheral slot of the standard Apple II computer. The second Sweet Talker board is designed for interfacing to any computer's TTL parallel ports. Since the Sweet Talker units utilize the Votrax phonetic synthesis chip, their capabilities may be found in the next section

The original Sweet Talker design was created by Steve Ciarcia and described in the September 1981 issue of *Byte Magazine*. The parallel version of the Sweet Talker circuit board is shown in Fig. 7-22 to illustrate the circuit board size and simplicity of its contents. Power required for the synthesizer module consists of +12-volt and +5-volt supplies. Both circuit boards contain audio filters and power amplifiers with volume controls for directly driving the output loudspeakers. Since both forms of the Sweet Talker are phoneme driven, their vocabulary is unlimited due to phonetic concatenation of words.

---

*Votrax is a registered trademark of Votrax® Div. of Federal Screw Works

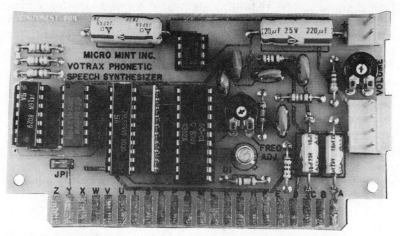

Fig. 7-22. The Micromint Sweet Talker phonetic synthesizer board. *(Courtesy Micromint, Inc.)*

VOTRAX SC-01 PHONEME SPEECH SYNTHESIZER CHIP

The SC-01 speech synthesizer manufactured by Votrax is a completely self-contained solid state integrated circuit. The design of the single chip synthesizer phonetically synthesizes continuous speech from input strings of phonemes. Contained within the SC-01 speech synthesizer chip are 64 individual and different phonemes, each of which is accessed by a 6-bit code. By properly selecting the sequence of phonemes for input to the synthesizer, the output will phonetically recreate the desired speech patterns.

The flow diagram of the 22-pin SC-01 synthesizer chip is shown in Fig. 7-23. This diagram illustrates the *lack* of complex connections to a driving computer interface. Six bits of input are used to address a desired phoneme within the chip while two bits select the pitch for the selected phoneme. If these inputs are driven at a rate of approximately 70 bits per second, the synthesizer chip will speak. Since the design of the integrated circuit is based upon CMOS techniques, the total current drain during operation is only 9 mA. This feature combined with the TTL compatible inputs makes this an ideal chip for interfacing to any home computer.

The actual operation of the synthesizer internal to the integrated circuit is very similar to the formant synthesizers de-

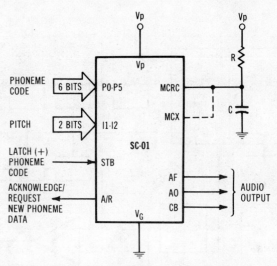

Fig. 7-23. The Votrax® SC-01 operational flow. *(Courtesy Votrax Corp. © 1980)*

scribed in Chapter 6. The block diagram of the chip shown in Fig. 7-24 can be compared directly with those in the previous chapter to identify the various component blocks. A visible difference between these two comparisons is the serial connection of the formant filters F1, F2, F3, and F4, rather than parallel connections. The effective results are the same, however.

In addition to supplying the individual synthesizer chip, Votrax also supplies several modules which utilize the SC-01 for speech generation. The first of these speech synthesizer modules is the Speech PAC™* (Phoneme Access Controller) module. This is a relatively low-cost, self-contained system which utilizes the low bit rate of the SC-01 with on-board storage of phoneme sequences and words to generate speech. The design of the phoneme access controller allows the system to store words accessible in eight byte increments. The capability for an on-board 2716 EPROM provides up to 255 vocabulary words of storage. In addition to being used in the stored vocabulary mode, the phoneme access controller may also be directly accessed for externally input phonetic speech. This gives the system the ability to speak with an unlimited vocabulary.

---

*Speech PAC and VSM/1 are trademarks of Votrax® Div. of Federal Screw Works

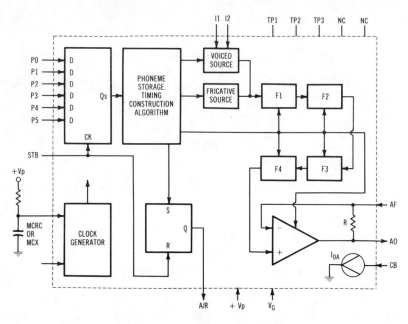

Fig. 7-24. Internal block diagram—Votrax® SC-01.

Fig. 7-25. The Votrax® SPEECH PAC™ synthesizer module. *(Courtesy Votrax® Div. Federal Screw Works)*

The block diagram of the phoneme access controller module shown in Fig. 7-26 illustrates the contents of the circuit board. Connections may be made directly through several parallel ports to create phonetic speech. Contained on the Speech PAC module is an audio amplifier designed to directly drive a loudspeaker.

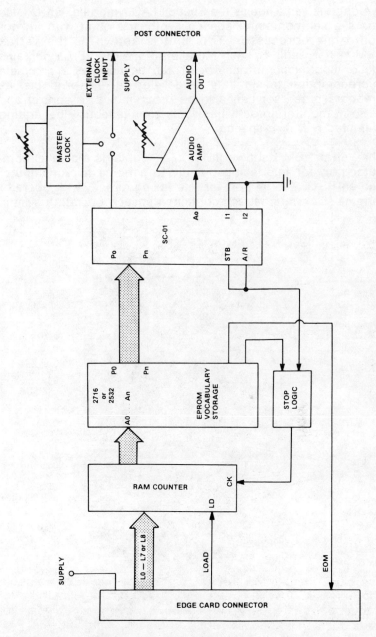

Fig. 7-26. The SPEECH PAC™ internal diagram. *(Courtesy Votrax® Div. Federal Screw Works)*

155

Along the same line as the Speech PAC™ module, Votrax also offers a self-contained speech synthesizer unit with an on-board microprocessor. This unit is known as the Votrax VSM/1™ (Versatile Speech Module). Since the VSM/1 contains the on-board microprocessor, it can be used as a complete microcomputer to simulate or develop talking products. Its on-board processor can also be programmed to control and perform monitoring activities while simultaneously generating unlimited real time speech.

The Votrax VSM/1 shown in Fig. 7-27 contains a parallel computer port for interfacing directly to a home microcomputer and an RS-232 serial port for interfacing directly with operator terminals. An internal self-contained speech operating system

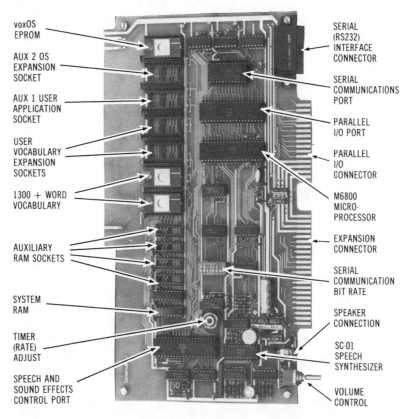

voxOS
EPROM

AUX 2 OS
EXPANSION
SOCKET

AUX 1 USER
APPLICATION
SOCKET

USER
VOCABULARY
EXPANSION
SOCKETS

1300 + WORD
VOCABULARY

AUXILIARY
RAM SOCKETS

SYSTEM
RAM

TIMER
(RATE)
ADJUST

SPEECH AND
SOUND EFFECTS
CONTROL PORT

SERIAL
(RS232)
INTERFACE
CONNECTOR

SERIAL
COMMUNICATIONS
PORT

PARALLEL
I/O PORT

PARALLEL
I/O
CONNECTOR

M6800
MICRO-
PROCESSOR

EXPANSION
CONNECTOR

SERIAL
COMMUNICATION
BIT RATE

SPEAKER
CONNECTION

SC-01
SPEECH
SYNTHESIZER

VOLUME
CONTROL

Fig. 7-27. The Votrax® VSM/1™ microcomputer speech module. *(Courtesy Votrax® Div. Federal Screw Works)*

known as VOXOS produces the speech operation for the system. Visible in the photograph of the VSM/1 are empty sockets for expansion of both the speech operating system and the self-contained vocabulary. Obviously, the capabilities of this speech synthesis module are quite powerful because of the self-contained microprocessor (the M6800).

The block diagram of the single board computer/speech synthesizer unit shown in Fig. 7-28 illustrates the powerful capabilities of the peripheral circuitry around the original SC-01 speech synthesizer chip. When this amount of computing power is placed around a speech synthesizer, the capabilities are almost unlimited. The user controllable software and vocabulary storage is quite large, allowing for complex custom applications. Existing within the internal operating software, a program allows for computer-to-computer transfer of spoken commands which in effect creates a "spooling" of the speech output. This allows the master computer to operate its synthesis peripheral much like a buffered printer. Although the cost of this unit is relatively high compared to most home speech synthesis peripheral modules, its use in commercial applications can prove very cost effective.

The capabilities of the VSM/1 allow for an internal vocabulary storage of over 1300 words. In addition, sound effects and variable stored sound macro instructions are permitted. Although this system does not have an internal text-to-speech capability, its applications are innumerable. Since Votrax *has* developed the text/speech capability in a stand alone module referred to as the "Type'N Talk"* speech synthesizer, it will be described separately in the following product description.

THE VOTRAX TYPE 'N TALK™ SPEECH SYNTHESIZER

The Type 'N Talk™* synthesizer from Votrax is a combination of previous products with an internal text-to-speech algorithm. As shown in Fig. 7-29, the Type 'N and Talk is designed as a stand alone synthesizer peripheral for any home computer system. It has an internal power supply and operates entirely through a serial RS-232C port. Two modes of operation are allowed for generating speech: (1) direct English text input and (2) direct phoneme input.

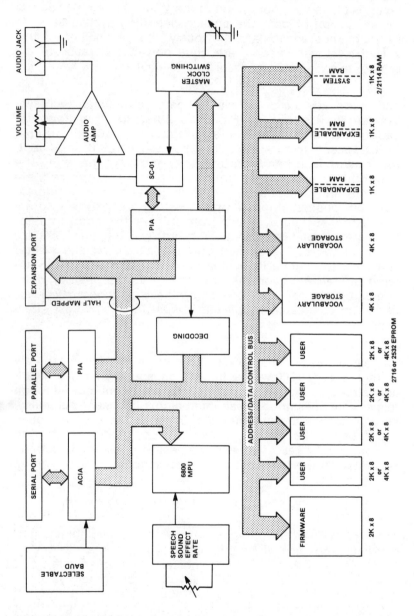

Fig. 7-28. The Votrax® VSM/1™ internal block diagram. *(Courtesy Votrax® Div. Federal Screw Works)*

158

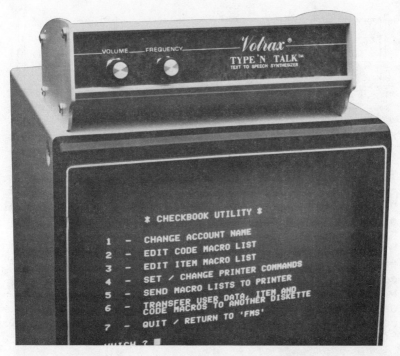

Fig. 7-29. TYPE 'N TALK™ speech synthesizer. *(Courtesy Votrax® Div. Federal Screw Works)*

Since the Type 'N Talk has its own internal microprocessor controller and 750 character buffer memory, even the smallest computers can be used to create unlimited vocabulary speech. The ease of use of the Type 'N Talk to generate speech is similar to using a serial line printer. In fact, the synthesizer system may be connected directly through a serial printer port to create speech rather than printed text.

The simplicity of the connections between the Type 'N Talk and your home computer is illustrated in Fig. 7-30. The rear panel computer connections and controls are clearly shown. The on/off power switch and power cord connector are at the left of the rear panel. In the center of the rear panel is the RS-232 serial port connector and a baud select switch which allows selection of baud rates from 75 to 9600 baud. At the far right of the rear panel is the speaker connection plug which connects to any standard 8-ohm speaker.

Fig. 7-30. Computer connections—TYPE 'N TALK™ (Courtesy Votrax® Div. Federal Screw Works)

The internal configuration of the Type 'N Talk synthesizer is quite proprietary to Votrax and consequently very little information is available on the actual circuitry. A block diagram, however, illustrates the basic internal workings from a conceptual standpoint. This is shown in Fig. 7-31. This illustrates that the system can be configured as an echoing peripheral (transparent) or as a direct computer-controlled interface. In either case, the RS-232 serial data from the computer is stored in the text input buffer with the capability of 750 characters. As the data is being input to the system, the text-to-speech translator converts the English text to phoneme control codes for the SC-01 speech synthesizer chip. The phonetically generated

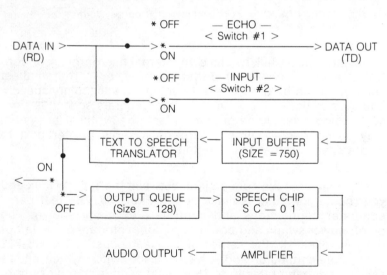

Fig. 7-31. Block diagram—Votrax® TYPE 'N TALK™ (Courtesy Votrax® Div. Federal Screw Works)

speech is then amplified and output through the audio output loudspeaker. The complexity of the software within the Type 'N Talk unit allows the synthesizer to receive phonemes or text, to echo the input, or to accept upper and lower case information in different contexts.

The specifications for the Votrax Type 'N Talk are shown in Chart 7-1. These show the operating capabilities and requirements for the system with any home computer. This is a very simple and powerful speech synthesizer which utilizes formant synthesis synthetic speech. It provides an unlimited vocabulary for home applications and has the characteristic robotic sound of formant speech synthesis.

Digital Vocal Tract Modeling Synthesizers

The commercial speech synthesizers described in this section all use the digital modeling of the vocal tract to create synthetic speech. The primary types of speech synthesis in this category are LPC and PARCOR speech. The LPC speech synthesizers

Chart 7-1. Type 'N Talk Specifications

PHYSICAL
Width . . . . .7.7 inches (19.3 mm)
Depth . . . . .5.2 inches (12.3 mm)
Height . . . . .3.1 inches (6.5 mm)
Weight . . . . .2 lbs. (0.896 Kg.)

Environment

Temperature . . . . .Operating:		40 to 100 degrees F
		(4 to 38 degrees C)
	Storage:	−35 to 150 degrees F
		(−37 to 65 degrees C)
Humidity . . . . .Operating:		20% to 90% (no condensation)
	Storage:	5% to 95% (no condensation)

Electrical

Power . . . . .Input to transformer*		120 V ac, 60 Hz, 20 W
	Input to TNT*	—pins 1-3, 26 V ac, 180 mA
(see note below)		—pin 2, 20 V dc, 50 mA
		—pin 4 is 0 volt reference
Interface . . . . .RS-232C compatible, 75-9600 baud		
	Frame bits = 1 start, 8 data, 1 stop	
Audio . . . . .1 watt into 8-ohm speaker, ac coupled		

*Use Only Votrax Approved Transformer Part No. 01p-1224B

Courtesy Votrax, Div. of Federal Screw Works.

are being developed primarily within the United States, while the PARCOR method is under investigation in Japan. One of the major product hurdles that the Japanese must overcome to effectively market their products in the United States is the generation of correctly spoken English for their vocabulary ROMs. This is a situation unique to the speech synthesis field. While the Japanese may learn to read and write English more fluently than those of us in the United States, it's highly unlikely that their spoken English speech would be accepted in any of our vocabulary ROM systems. Thus, the vocabulary used within their systems must come from either American speakers or Japanese speakers without a Japanese accent.

The speech synthesis products listed in Table 7-5 are currently available through the manufacturers named. See Appendix C for addresses. Although the type of speech synthesis utilized is primarily LPC, the PARCOR method is also mentioned to indicate that there is considerable activity in this area. (The PARCOR method is very similar in its technique to LPC.)

This list is expected to grow most rapidly over the next few years. Linear predictive coded speech is becoming a powerful contender in the field of speech synthesis because of its efficiency and low data rate requirements. It also possesses a speech quality approaching that of recorded speech.

HITACHI HD61885; HD38880,1,2

Although the Hitachi speech synthesis products are not readily available over the counter to the average computerist, they are presented here to show you what's happening in the field of PARCOR generated speech. Hitachi has two basic types of speech synthesizers available in integrated circuit form. The first of these is the HD61885, a one-chip CMOS speech synthesis integrated circuit. Contained in the 28-pin integrated circuit is a PARCOR speech synthesizer and 32K bit ROM for speech storage. In addition, the digital-to-analog converter and keyboard input interface are also included. The on-chip ROM has the capability for 26 seconds of speech. Under average conditions, this will provide up to a 63-word vocabulary. The addition of external read only memories to the synthesis chip adds approximately 100 seconds of speech per ROM. Since 16 ROMs can be added to the synthesizer, a very large vocabulary or speech capability can be created with this synthesizer.

Table 7-5. Currently Available LPC Type Speech Synthesizers.

Company	Synthesis Type	Size	Speech Capability	Computer Type	Cost
1. Hitachi HD61885,	PARCOR 10-Pole	28 Pin DIP	Custom ROM Speech	Any	
HD38880, 1, 2	PARCOR 10-Pole	42 Pin DIP			
2. Street Electronics ECHO II & ECHO-GP	10-Pole LPC (T.I.) 10-Pole LPC (T.I.)	APPLE II Card, 2×7×5 in (5×17.8×12.7 cm)	Phoneme-LPC Text-to-Speech	APPLE II, (ECHO II) Any (ECHO-GP)	$200 $370
3. Speech Technology Corp. M410, VR/S100	12-Pole LPC	4×4-in P.C. Card (10.2×10.2 cm)	Standard Vocabulary	Any (M410)	$185
	12-Pole LPC	5×10-in P.C. Card (12.7×25.4 cm)	ROMs	S-100 Bus (VR/S100)	$325
4. Telesensory Speech Systems Speech 1000	12-Pole LPC	7×12-in (17.8×30.5 cm) P.C. Card	Vocabulary ROM	RS-232; PARALLEL TTL	$1200
SP1020	12-Pole LPC	17×18×3-in (43.2×45.7×7.6 cm)	Vocabulary ROM	Any; RS-232	$2500
Prose 2000™	12-Pole LPC	7×12-in (17.8×30.5 cm) P.C. Card	Text-to-Speech	Any RS-232, Multibus	$3500
5. Texas Instruments Speak and Spell	10-Pole LPC	8×12×2-in (20.3×30.5×5 cm)	200 + Word Vocabulary	6502 Microprocessor	$60.00
TMS 5200 PASS™	10-Pole LPC LPC Encoder	28 Pin DIP Portable	External ROM Real Time Speech-to-LPC	N/A	$80.00 ≈15,000

163

A second type of speech synthesis integrated circuit also available from Hitachi is referred to as the HD38880 integrated circuit speech synthesizer. This synthesizer like the HD61885 operates using the PARCOR method of LPC speech but is constructed with a PMOS type of silicon integration. The primary difference is that this type of synthesizer construction requires more power than the CMOS version. The speech storage capability of this synthesizer (on chip) is the same as the CMOS version. In fact, other than the method of silicon integration, there is very little difference between these two synthesis products. In operation and internal complexity, these synthesizers are very similar to the LPC synthesis products described in the remainder of this section. Further information on Hitachi products may be obtained by writing directly to the manufacturer.

STREET ELECTRONICS, CORP. ECHO II™ AND ECHO-GP™

The ECHO™ series synthesizers marketed by Street Electronics Corporation are probably the first available home computer LPC speech synthesizers. The heart of the ECHO synthesizers is the Texas Instruments TMS-5200 speech processor. Two versions of the ECHO synthesizers are currently being marketed by SEC: The ECHO II and the ECHO-GP. The ECHO II speech synthesis module shown in Fig. 7-32 illustrates the compact-

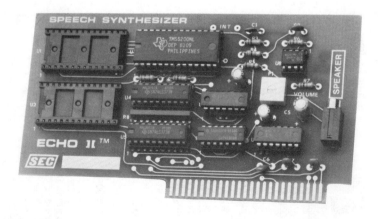

Fig. 7-32. Echo™ LPC speech synthesizer. *(Courtesy Street Electronics Corp.)*

ness of the speaking peripheral for the Apple II computer. At the left of the circuit board are two empty ROM sockets which provide for on-board vocabulary storage. Since the ECHO series synthesizers utilize phonetic LPC speech, this line of synthesizers has an unlimited vocabulary, characteristic of the formant synthesizers. It also exhibits the similar robotic sound which stems from its use of the phoneme concatenation.

One of the really nice features of phonetic LPC synthesis is that the phoneme stringing mode can be combined with the direct recorded LPC speech mode. This allows you to create a very natural sound for common words and convert to the phoneme mode of speech generation during custom speech.

In addition, Street Electronics has included within the ECHO synthesizers, a text parsing program known as the Textalker™. This program takes standard ASCII output from, for instance, a PRINT statement and converts it directly to speech. Since the Textalker contains almost 400 rules for English pronunciation, it will correctly pronounce 96% of the thousand most commonly used words in English. The exceptions to the spoken English words can be corrected in two manners using the Textalker program. The first method of pronunciation correction is the deliberate misspelling of a word in order to fool the synthesizer into a correct pronunciation. This is simply spelling the word exactly like it sounds. And in many cases where there is a silent letter within the word, the word is pronounced most correctly when the silent word is omitted from the ASCII text input. An example might be to correctly pronounce the word "label;" the word would be deliberately misspelled "layble."

In addition to the text-to-speech capabilities, the ECHO series synthesizers also have the facilities for direct input of phoneme speech. This mode of speaking is slightly more difficult because you have to piece together the words phonetically. In many cases, however, this is the only way to correctly pronounce unusually spelled words.

The capabilities for text-to-speech and phonetic speech also exist within the ECHO-GP synthesizer manufactured by Street Electronics Corporation. This enclosed system contains an internal microprocessor and may be used as a stand alone speech synthesizer. Interface connections to any computer using the ECHO-GP synthesizer may be serial RS-232 or parallel TTL. Operating controls on the ECHO-GP synthesizer shown in Fig. 7-33 are extremely simple consisting only of a power on/off switch and a volume control. The use of this synthesizer is basically the same as the ECHO II model for the Apple II computer, except that this synthesizer is designed for a universal interface to any home computer. Its capabilities for speaking are the same, including the Textalker program for generating text-to-speech output. The included microprocessor that comes with the GP model takes much of the housekeeping work from your computer while generating synthetic speech. The added cost for the internal intelligence is certainly a bargain.

Fig. 7-33. Echo™ GP LPC speech synthesizer. *(Courtesy Street Electronics Corp.)*

SPEECH TECHNOLOGY CORPORATION M410 AND VR/S100

The products manufactured by Speech Technology Corporation utilize the General Instruments LPC synthesizer chip. This is not surprising considering the fact that the people at Speech Technology worked very closely with General Instruments to actually design the circuit.

The M410 speech generator module contains a 12-pole LPC speech synthesizer circuit. The relatively small board shown in Fig. 7-34 interfaces to a parallel TTL computer port of any microprocessor or microcomputer system. The module has the capability for an on-board vocabulary of up to 120 words and a self-contained audio amplifier for driving an 8-ohm loudspeaker. It also has its own internally programmed 8039 microprocessor for controlling the voice peripheral chip. Vocabularies for the M410 may be purchased from Speech Technology Corporation in 2716 or 2732 EPROMs. In addition to the stan-

OUTPUT
LEVEL ADJUST

OPTIONAL COMPONENTS
FOR MATCHED TELEPHONE
LINE OR 8-OHM SPEAKER

AUDIO, POWER, AND CONTROL
SIGNALS WITH 20-PIN FLAT
CABLE CONNECTION

SOCKETS FOR 2716/2732
EPROM VOCABULARIES TO
120 WORDS

Fig. 7-34. The M410 Speech Generator module. *(Courtesy Speech Technology Corp.)*

dard vocabulary words, Speech Technology Corporation will also encode custom vocabularies for any of their speech systems at additional cost.

To examine the complexity of the on-board electronics in the M410 speech generator, look at Fig. 7-35. Although the major portion of this schematic diagram is the microprocessor and associated memory components, the speech synthesizer chip (U5) is shown with its interface to the microprocessor and audio output amplifier. The program for the 8039 microprocessor CPU is stored within the EPROM memory and occupies approximately the first 900 bytes of storage. Above that address location, vocabulary data may be stored. This is a very powerful speech synthesis peripheral for its size.

A second speech synthesizer peripheral offered by Speech Technology Corporation is the VR/S100 speech generator. This

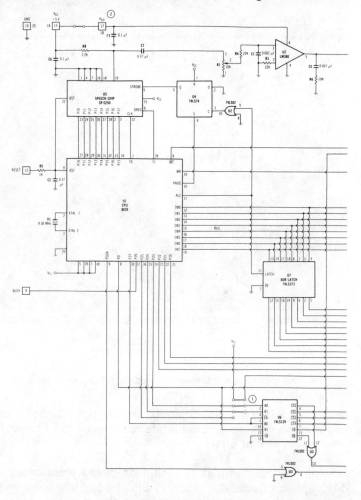

Fig. 7-35. Speech circuitry—M410 Speech

is a larger module designed for the S-100 bus configuration with approximately the same capabilities as the M410. A significant difference between the two units is the VR/S100 can operate up to two synthetic speech chips for dual-speech outputs from a single board. This allows the capability of two simultaneous speech outputs with different messages for such applications as multiple telephone line systems. The VR/S100 printed circuit board, shown in Fig. 7-36, contains an on-board 8085 microprocessor to interface with the controlling microcomputer and the speech synthesizer integrated circuit. The

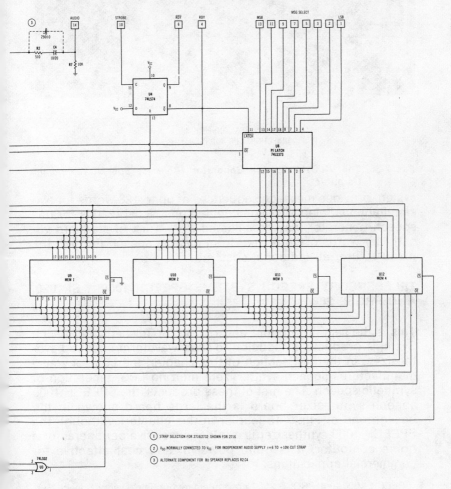

Generator. *(Courtesy Speech Technology Corp.)*

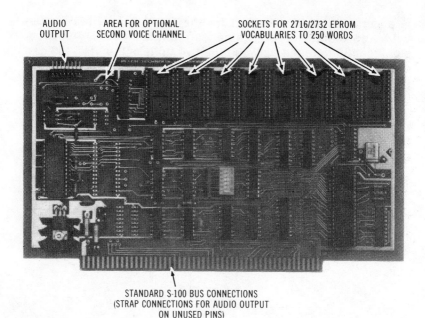

AUDIO OUTPUT   AREA FOR OPTIONAL SECOND VOICE CHANNEL   SOCKETS FOR 2716/2732 EPROM VOCABULARIES TO 250 WORDS

STANDARD S-100 BUS CONNECTIONS
(STRAP CONNECTIONS FOR AUDIO OUTPUT
ON UNUSED PINS)

Fig. 7-36. The VR/S100 Speech Generator. *(Courtesy Speech Technology Corp.)*

system provides message sequences of up to 128 words for two simultaneous telephone line connections. Vocabularies for this speech generator may be selected from a list of standard vocabulary words or generated from custom speech through the manufacturer at additional cost.

TELESENSORY SPEECH SYSTEMS SPEECH 1000™, SP1020, AND PROSE 2000™*

This is the second product description for Telesensory Speech Systems products. In addition to their waveform encoded synthesizers in the first section of this chapter, the company also manufactures speech synthesizers utilizing LPC generation of synthetic speech. The first of these products, the SPEECH 1000 speech synthesizer board is the large board shown in the background of Fig. 7-15 (earlier in this chapter). Although the SPEECH 1000 synthesizer is a rather expensive peripheral for a home computer, it is quite powerful and cost effective for commercial applications.

---

*SPEECH 1000 and PROSE 2000 are trademarks of Telesensory Speech Systems Div. of Telesensory Systems, Inc.

The LPC synthesis method employed by the SPEECH 1000 uses a 12-pole lattice filter to produce the digital model of the vocal tract. And, since the synthesizer board contains an on-board 8085A microprocessor, it has the intelligence to respond to external commands and execute the speech output independently from the primary computer. The block diagram of the circuitry on the SPEECH 1000 board is shown in Fig. 7-37. This shows that the board contains a truly flexible and versatile high performance speech synthesizer. It can synthesize multiple voices, male or female, in one language or many.

The SPEECH 1000 synthesizer may operate in an interrupt driven or polled command mode. It interfaces over a multibus interface *or* parallel port for 8-bit parallel TTL information. There is also a standard RS-232C serial port for creating speech output. Since the on-board memory capability is 458 kilobits of storage, the SPEECH 1000 board will talk for almost 200 seconds without repeating itself. The vocabulary for the synthesizer may be obtained either from a standard vocabulary list or through custom encoding of vocabulary words from Telesensory Speech Systems.

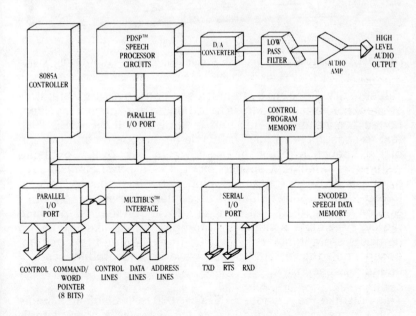

Fig. 7-37. **Inside the SPEECH 1000™.** *(Courtesy Telesensory Speech Systems)*

The SPEECH 1000 synthesizer board may also be purchased as a stand alone response unit, including power supply, cabinet, and electronic computer interface. This unit in known as the SP1020 speech peripheral. The self-contained LPC speech synthesizer shown in Fig. 7-38 is basically the SPEECH 1000 synthesizer board designed for stand alone operation. The flexibility of this system, with it RS-232C serial communications interface, can certainly be exploited for many commercial applications. For a demonstration of the quality of speech from the SPEECH 1000 synthesizer call the Telesensory Speech Systems demonstration number (at your expense). This number which was mentioned previously in the waveform encoded products from Telesensory Systems is a direct computer interface to the telephone line rather than a recording. It allows you to choose the synthesizer products by keying in numbers from your telephone dial. The TSS demonstration number (which is *not* toll-free) is (415) 856-0225.

Fig. 7-38. The SP1020 LPC synthesizer containing the SPEECH 1000™ board.
(Courtesy Telesensory Speech Systems)

Telesensory Speech Systems also manufactures a text-to-speech converter system in addition to the previously mentioned two products. This unit is known as the PROSE 2000 text-to-speech converter. The single circuit board configuration of the speech synthesizer is shown in Fig. 7-39. Contained within this intelligent speech module is a proprietary speech synthesis-by-rule program developed by Telesensory Systems to provide a virtually unlimited vocabulary. The system operates by converting ASCII coded text into allophones to produce highly intelligible speech. In addition, human-like intonation contours are automatically derived from the input text and imposed upon the output speech waveform to produce natural sounding speech.

This unit, like the previous SPEECH 1000 is available in a single board format or packaged in an enclosure with a power supply

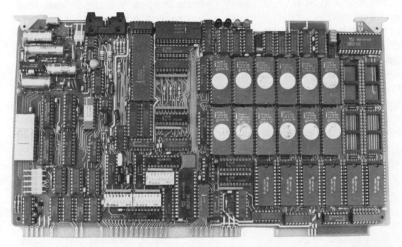

Fig. 7-39. The PROSE™ **2000 text-to-speech convertor board.** *(Courtesy Tele-sensory Speech Systems)*

and appropriate connectors. The interface to the host computer may be through a serial RS-232 port since the converter board contains its internal *8086* microprocessor. The data rates required for speaking are as low as 100 bits per second. The quality of the direct text-to-speech spoken output from the PROSE 2000 may be observed by dialing the previously mentioned demonstration number. Further information on these rather complex products may be obtained directly from Telesensory Speech Systems.

TEXAS INSTRUMENTS SPEAK AND SPELL™*

Although it may seem strange seeing this device being listed as a speech synthesis peripheral, it can be done. Several companies have produced interface units which allow the Speak and Spell to be interfaced to home computer ports. Since the Texas Instruments learning aid was one of the first commercial products to utilize LPC generation of speech, it was quickly exploited as an available speech synthesizer.

The circuitry within the Speak and Spell contains the TMS5100 speech synthesis chip and a custom version of the TMS-1000 4-bit microprocessor. Since Texas Instruments had the fore-

---

*Speak and Spell™ is a trademark of Texas Instruments.

173

sight to include a vocabulary expansion port on the Speak and Spell circuit board, hardware experimenters have designed and produced interface circuits for directly connecting the Speak and Spell to several types of computers. This port is at the upper right of Fig. 7-40; the Speak and Spell schematic.

One type of peripheral interface converter for the Speak and Spell is manufactured by the Percom Data Company, 211 N. Kirby, Garland, Texas 75042. This unit is designed to interface to the TRS-80 through the expansion port and drive the Speak and Spell with its internal vocabulary. Each word within the vocabulary may be externally accessed and spoken through

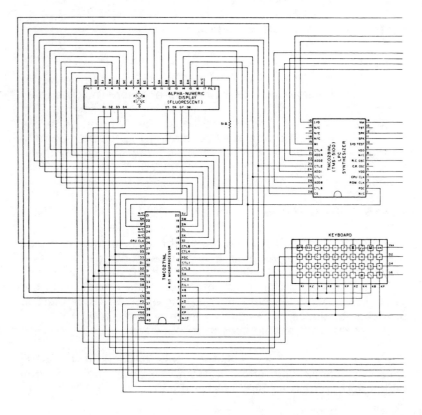

Fig. 7-40. The Texas Instruments'

peek or poke commands. While the combination of the Percom Speak-2-Me-2™ and the Texas Instruments Speak and Spell provides a very low cost LPC speech synthesis interface, there is a lack of practical everyday words in the resident Speak and Spell vocabulary. By applying the additional vocabulary expansion modules with the existing interface, some of those missing words can be generated.

Another manufacturer of Speak and Spell interface modules is East Coast MicroProducts, 1307 Beltram Court, Odenton, Maryland. This interface module, unlike the Percom system, gives away the secrets of its operation and allows you not only to

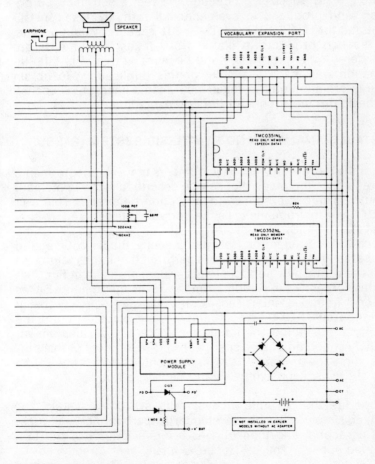

Speak-and-Spell schematic.

control the Speak and Spell output, but read its vocabulary into memory. This interface is designed primarily for 6502 microprocessors, and interfaces through a parallel 6522 port. The instruction manual supplied with the East Coast MicroProducts interface board is quite complete and allows the experimenter to delve into the workings of a low-cost speech synthesis peripheral.

TEXAS INSTRUMENTS TMS5200

Among the numerous products for generating LPC speech that are available from Texas Instruments, the TMS5200 speech processor chip is probably the most important. This is the heart of the LPC synthesizer produced by Street Electronics Corporation, and produced in evaluation kit form by Texas Instruments as the TMSK101 and TMSK201 speech evaluation kits. The speech products available from Texas Instruments are considered quite proprietary and because of this, very little information was made available for this publication. To obtain more information on the Texas Instruments line of LPC speech synthesis products, contact the company directly.

PORTABLE ANALYSIS AND SYNTHESIS SYSTEM (PASS)

One of the more important developments that Texas Instruments has recently announced that *can* be described is the implementation of a portable speech-to-LPC code generator. This unit which Texas Instruments calls the portable analysis and synthesis system (PASS) is a prototype design of a true real time speech-to-LPC generator. Until just recently, the task of creating LPC parameters from speech was performed in large mainframe computers. The new portable PASS system is shown in Fig. 7-41 courtesy of Mr. Steve Roubik from the Texas Instruments Dallas Regional Training Center. These units, that will eventually cost in the range of $10,000, are expected to be placed around the country at the various regional training centers for custom vocabulary encoding of LPC speech. The development of this portable, high speed system is of monumental significance in the field of LPC speech synthesis and generation code.

To operate the portable analysis and synthesis system, the speaker simply talks into a standard microphone, waits less than a second, and then obtains a digital output of the LPC encoded speech. The LPC code is finally sent directly via the RS-232 serial port to a computer or printer. The PASS system

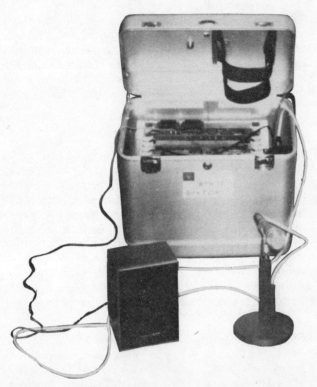

Fig. 7-41. The Texas Instruments' PASS LPC encoding system.

also contains an LPC synthesizer which allows the user to review the spoken message before obtaining the equivalent LPC codes. As this system becomes more widely available, the popularity of LPC speech synthesizers is sure to increase. This is the first available portable system for real time speech encoding directly to LPC parameters.

This concludes the review of products in this section. Although other products may currently be entering the market, their omission is not intentional. The field of speech synthesis is moving so fast that if a book could be published in one day, there would probably still be omissions. You have, however, seen the major contenders in today's market.

Now that we have seen the synthesizers and how they work, let's examine the subject that should be of primary concern to anyone considering the use of a speech synthesizer: applying the speech synthesis peripheral.

chapter 8

A Computer Speech Potpourri

The last remaining pertinent topic in this rather comprehensive coverage of the science of speech synthesis is that of application. In other words, what do you really plan to do with your synthetic speech system after you get it working? In this chapter we will consider a few possible applications for your talking system within your home and immediate surroundings and then venture off into some rather blue sky suggestions for talking systems that you might be the first to implement. Depending upon the complexity of the system you eventually create, you can use the ideas presented in this chapter to impress your family, friends, or colleagues; or just occupy your spare time and entertain yourself.

This chapter will be divided into three basic sections. The first will discuss a minimal speech system consisting of a home computer and speaking peripheral device. The second section involves the use of the home computer and speaking peripheral in conjunction with other computer peripheral devices around the home. A final section of this chapter describes possible commercial uses for speech synthesis products. Some of these commercial applications currently exist while others may be nearing reality in backroom laboratories. No matter how you decide to eventually apply your speech synthesizer, you will still get many, many hours of enjoyment from its use. After you meet the challenge of one particular application that you might have in mind, then you will probably want to go on to more complex experiments. Remember, this is still a very young and growing field of electronics. Your particular application may be the very one to gain a patent and eventually make you rich and famous.

With those thoughts in mind, let's begin our search for synthetic speech applications with the basic computer/speech synthesis peripheral system. Although this is considered the minimum system, there are many uses and projects which can occupy your time and give you a better understanding of the capabilities of a speaking computer.

The Minimal System

After you have successfully spoken the first few words from your computer synthesis system, you will undoubtedly start thinking about possible intelligent uses for your new-found computer capabilities. The applications given in this section assume that you have the minimal system configuration as shown in Fig. 8-1. This system consists of the computer, its keyboard and display, and the speech synthesizer. While this doesn't appear to be a powerful system, there are numerous projects which you can start with this configuration. In fact, the number of projects is really limited only by your own imagination. However, just to give you the first spark, let's examine a few.

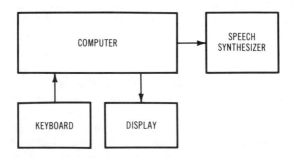

Fig. 8-1. A minimum synthetic speech system.

A TALKING CLOCK

This is one of the simplest speaking systems that you might devise which relies completely on software to produce its ef-

180

fect. It assumes that you have the capability for keeping time within your computer in the form of a time-of-day clock. If not, then you can still attempt this project by writing your own software timing loops to provide the necessary delays. The resultant effect of this project will be to create, with your computer and speech synthesizer, a clock which speaks the correct time upon command or at hourly intervals. The means by which this will be accomplished is a software program designed to keep the correct time of day and cue the speech synthesizer for spoken output as required.

The program for implementing the talking time-of-day clock can be written in either assembly language, BASIC, or other high level language, depending on your computer's capability. Of course, the first assumption is that your speech peripheral has the correct vocabulary for implementing the time-of-day functions. The minimum vocabulary for this project should consist of the words shown in Table 8-1. The table contains a total of 29 words which can completely describe the time of day at any individual minute. Since we would like the capability for not only announcing the hours, but also for outputting the correct time upon command, we need the speech capacity for counting and speaking up to the number 59. If your synthesizer is phoneme driven, then these words should be preencoded into phonemes before they can be spoken. If you have a type of synthesizer with an existing vocabulary, then find the command codes which will access each of the necessary time-of-day utterances. Once the initial vocabulary has been established within your system, then you may generate the program to produce the talking clock system.

Table 8-1. The Talking Clock Vocabulary

the	thirteen
time	fourteen
is	fifteen
(pause)	sixteen
one	seventeen
two	eighteen
three	nineteen
four	twenty
five	thirty
six	forty
seven	fifty
eight	oh
nine	clock
ten	
eleven	
twelve	

A flowchart for a possible talking clock program is given in Fig. 8-2. Although this program is shown in general terms, it is specific enough that the illustrated decision blocks can be simply converted to your specific program language. While the program flow shown in Fig. 8-2 is relatively straightforward and simple, a slight difficulty exists when speaking the minutes of time, other than on the hour. For instance, if the hour time is automatically announced as "5 o'clock," then the number of hours spoken will never exceed 12. When a keyboard command is made to speak the time randomly, however, the spoken time might vary from 5:01 to 5:59 between 5 and 6 o'clock. A simple way to perform the vocabulary conversion from numbers to words might be to create a table with 60 numeric entries for minutes from 00 = o'clock to 59 = fifty-nine. In this way, the minutes can be directly accessed from computer memory and the vocabulary words pulled out for synthesizer activation. Those of you lucky enough to have a text-to-speech conversion program in your synthesizer probably won't have to bother with any of this numeric conversion. Most of these text conversion programs have the internal ability to determine how numbers from 1 to 100 are spoken, based solely on a numeric input. In this case, all that you should have to provide to your speech synthesizer as a command for spoken time is the numeric time of day. The text-to-speech algorithm will handle the pronunciation of the minutes. Some text-to-speech algorithms are so intelligent that they can even tell that the number they are receiving from the computer is time because the first digits are separated from the second by a colon. This synthesizer, given the text string "5:22", would pronounce the time as "five . . . twenty-two."

This rather simple experiment can be easily tried with any computer having the capability for reading an internal clock which keeps the time of day. In some computers, this may be accomplished through the time$ function. In others, with hardware clocks, reading time consists of reading the clock chip peripheral ports. If you have neither of these in your computer, then you might start by creating a timing loop with a very accurate timing of one loop per second. Within this loop, a divide by 60 counting loop should be implemented to keep track of the minute marks. At each minute mark, another counting loop of 60 should be advanced to track the minutes over an hour's time. And finally, a counting loop of 12 should be advanced by each cycle of the 60-minute counter to track the hours. The numeric output from all of these loops can be used to tell the

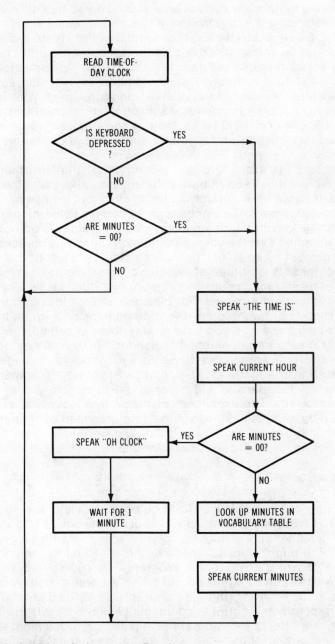

Fig. 8-2. A talking clock program flowchart.

183

speaking system the correct time of day. If you had difficulty in understanding the description of that software clock, then look at Fig. 8-3. It illustrates a rather simple way to create a time-of-day clock in software for driving the speech program. The implementation of this software system in a talking computer can provide a very impressive demonstration of synthetic speech capabilities because the system no longer relies on your direct input to create each individual spoken word. Your talking clock will continue to tell time as long as the program runs with a continual updating of the spoken time throughout the day.

If we take the example of the talking clock a little further and add some time-recognition software into the overall timing loop, then we have not only a talking clock but we can program certain phrases to be announced at certain times or possibly even dates. With a little creativity, a talking alarm clock can be programmed to wake you up in the morning with a phrase such as "get out of bed" or "get up, stupid, it's late." If you have appointments or times at which you must remember something, these times could be programmed into the system with the appropriate message. For instance, at 6 o'clock in the evening you might want to have your computer say "turn on the tv. It's time for news." If you have a rather busy schedule, then you might create an appointment calendar which lists each day's activities and announces these to you while you are getting dressed in the morning. The beauty of this system is that it is extremely reliable and will never forget to remind you of your commitments. The usefulness of the system for a busy person would be well justified. The verbal reinforcement of hearing the upcoming day's activities each morning would surely eliminate the possibility of missed appointments.

FUN AND GAMES

The previous example was just one possible use of the minimal speech synthesis system. As you begin to gain more knowledge and become more familiar with your speech synthesis peripheral, you might want to integrate the speaking capability into some of your favorite game programs. Of course, this will require an intimate knowledge of the programs that you will modify. If, however, they are written in BASIC, then you can often identify the "print" statements (which normally are used for game interaction) and either replace or supplement these printed output statements with verbal messages. One of the more popular games on which verbal response is quite effec-

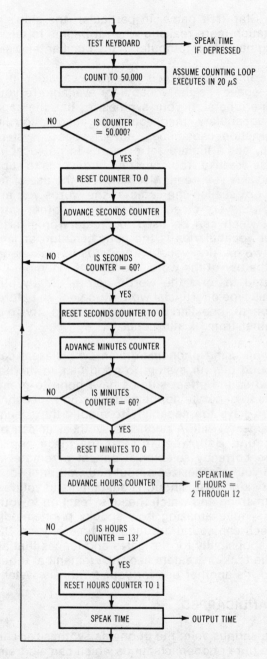

Fig. 8-3. A possible software time-of-day clock program.

tive is the Star Trek game. In particular, the ship's computer becomes much more realistic when it begins to talk to you as did the original ship's computer in the familiar television series.

One of the limitations which you must consider in modifying games for speech is the vocabulary available to your speech synthesis peripheral. If your synthesizer has the capability for unlimited vocabulary, then your own imagination limits your game interaction capabilities. If your speech system, on the other hand, has a limited set of words in its vocabulary, then you must be creative. You can often find words to substitute for the missing one you need. Also consider the use of homonyms which are not spelled the same as the words you are looking for but sound very close or identical. Another rather crafty technique which can be used to create words missing from synthesizer vocabularies is the concatenation or jamming together of two existing vocabulary words to create another. For example, the use of the word "be" and the number "4" can be concatenated to form the word "before." Many other cases exist for this type of artificial word stringing, so before you give up hope on a nonexistent vocabulary word, try to piece the word together from existing ones.

Those of you using phoneme-driven synthesizers can put the robotic sound of your system to good use. In the past, movie studios and sound effect studios have gone to great expense and trouble to generate nonhuman sounding speech. With your system, you have the capability to modify the speech sounds and phonemes at will. A phoneme synthesizer can be very effective around Halloween time if the pitch and phoneme sounds are correctly selected. Connect a remote front door speaker to your synthesizer output and wait until you hear that familiar "trick or treat" shout. Then, command your synthesizer to speak anything and watch the kids' reaction to your artificial speech. It's quite amazing how spooky phoneme-driven synthetic speech can sound around that time of year. Of course, I take no responsibility for the gates and fences that are broken down as the trick-or-treaters flee. Just remember though, it's all in fun, *and* it's another use for your synthesis system.

AID TO HANDICAPPED

On a more serious vein, the phoneme synthesizer can be used to produce pure phonemic sounds which can aid tremendously in training persons with speech disabilities. With the simple capability for programming a phoneme and having it spoken continuously, you have at your disposal a tool which speech therapists have dreamed of for years. This teaching aid can be of tremendous help in correcting infant and young children's speech defects. If the concept is taken a step further and the phoneme synthesizer is used in conjunction with an available spectrograph for generating visible speech, deaf people can learn to create sounds which visibly match those from the synthesizer. By doing this, people who have never heard speech or spoken words can, by themselves, begin to acquire the ability for speech in the privacy of their home.

One of the most practical uses for the minimum system configuration allows blind and poorly sighted people to use the computer terminal. Since the problem of computer input for blind people has been effectively solved by Braille keyboards, they have very little trouble entering information into a computer. The computer's output is more of a problem and until just recently, only Braille printers have been effective in providing computer responses. Now, if a speech synthesizer is correctly configured to respond to all computer output data, including the keyboard echo, the unsighted individual will have the full power of the computer available to him. This will require, of course, a comprehensive text-to-speech algorithm program within the computer to provide the necessary unlimited vocabulary for computer output.

Most of the currently available phoneme-driven synthesizers have at least a rather simple text-to-speech algorithm available for the user. If you are not so fortunate to have this available for your system, then you might consider the generation of such a program as a challenge. There has been considerable work and research in this area, much of which is published. The following three references should provide considerable insight and help into the understanding and even writing of speech-by-rule algorithms for phonemic synthesizers:

M. D. McIlroy, "Synthetic English Speech by Rule," *Computer Science Technical Report 14,* Bell Telephone Laboratories, Murray Hill, NJ, March 1974.

H. Elowitz, et al, "Automatic Translation of English Text to Phonetics by means of Letter-to-Sound Rules," *Naval Research Laboratory Report 7948,* January 1976.

J. P. Allen, "Synthesis of Speech from Unrestricted Text," *Proceedings of the IEEE,* April 1976, 64(4), pp. 433–42.

If you have an interest in the text-to-speech algorithms as used in most phoneme synthesizers, these reports give you secrets as to their inner workings. The operation of these programs is very complex since there are thousands of exceptions to spoken English text. None of the speech-by-rule programs are perfect. Any major improvements in the existing algorithm programs would surely be greeted with universal acceptance.

AND SO ON

One last application for speech synthesis with the minimum configuration which I would like to suggest as a challenge is for someone to use his talking computer to teach a talking bird to speak. The computer can be used to repeatedly and monotonously say the same word again and again. This is ideal for teaching a feathered pet the English language. However, don't be surprised if your bird closely mimics the imperfections of your own synthesizer. After all, it is only repeating what it hears. It might even be possible to create a talking bird that sounds robotic. Can you imagine that?

These projects are not, by any means, the only ones which you can try with the minimum speech system. As stated earlier, the uses for this system are limited only by your imagination. The apparent intelligence of your synthesizer will improve greatly however, if you control its speaking from a program rather than from the keyboard. So get busy writing programs that speak. You might learn something about your system and have fun at the same time.

The Talking Home Computer with Peripherals

This section is dedicated to those of you who like to tinker. After you familiarize yourself with the minimal system configuration, you can really enhance the capabilities of your speaking computer by adding a few peripheral devices. Most of these can be supported with a few parallel or serial input/output ports. Although the uses presented in this section are primarily for around home, they can be extended through your own imagination to any place that you desire. You will find as you integrate your talking computer into the real world, that its usefulness is very impressive. Take, for example, the connection of your talking computer to your doorbell.

A TALKING DOORBELL

The diagram shown in Fig. 8-4 can be used to create a rather unusual talking doorbell, The only external components needed to implement this application are one or two small relays that should be wired in parallel with your doorbell solenoid coils. The relays should, of course, be the same voltage that your doorbell operates on, so be careful when choosing these components. The contacts of the relays can be wired to single-bit inputs of your computer's parallel input port. If you have a front and a rear doorbell button, then your computer could be wired to both as shown. If you have a single doorbell pushbutton, then you obviously need only the single relay and one input bit to your computer.

The vocal response that your computer gives upon the doorbell activation is up to you. You might, for instance, program it to say "someone is at the door." If you had a front and back doorbell, then you might have it say "someone is at the front door"

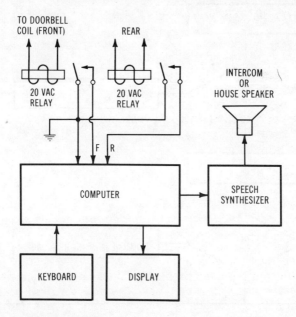

Fig. 8-4. A talking doorbell.

189

or "someone is at the back door." You will want to be sure to include an annunciator tone or sound before the speech begins as mentioned in Chapter 4 to remind the listeners of the up-coming speech. A possible program for implementing this rather simple home application is shown in the flowchart of Fig. 8-5. Although the program flow is extremely simple, the two blocks marked "Speak (Phrase)" should be programmed much like a "print" statement for your computer to respond to *"speak"* commands. The vocabulary should also be stored as two phrases to simplify the doorbell programming.

A TALKING HOME SECURITY SYSTEM

Another rather simple application of a talking computer in the home consists of a talking burglar alarm. Can you imagine the shock and surprise for an unwanted intruder if he heard "Bur-glary at the rear bedroom window—call the police!" Of course, other phrases could be used with the same effectiveness. The major scare to a burglar is that there is someone talking within

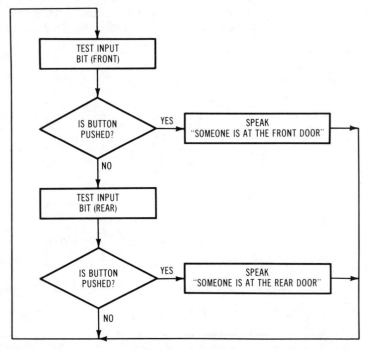

Fig. 8-5. A talking doorbell program flowchart.

the house. The hardware implementation of this system is shown in Fig. 8-6. The representative window and door contacts are simply the magnetic switches available at any local electronics or home security system store. Each magnetic switch is wired to one bit of the computer input port and remains closed until either the wire is cut, or the window or door is open. If a simple heat sensor is purchased or made and connected to another input port, then the system will also serve to warn the residents of a fire or heat build up in the residence. The fact that the computer can test the individual bits with a preprogrammed knowledge of which ones are burglary contacts and which ones are thermal contacts allows it to determine the ultimate message to be spoken. The flowchart of a simple home security program for servicing this configuration is given in Fig. 8-7. The operation of this program is very similar to the previous talking doorbell except that the messages are changed.

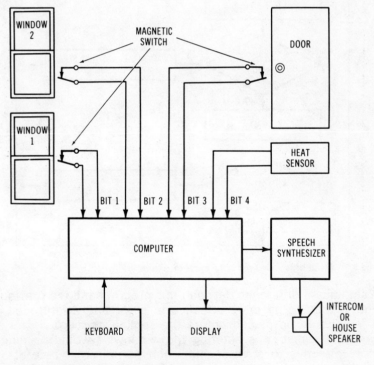

Fig. 8-6. A talking home security system.

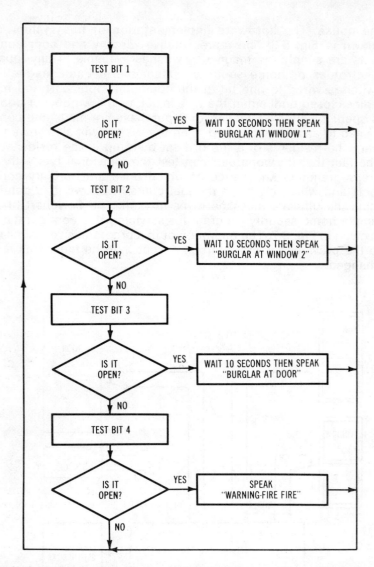

Fig. 8-7. A talking home security system example.

A significant difference between this program and the previous one is that, to be more effective in surprising an intruder, a delay should be placed before the spoken message. In other words, if someone is entering the window, it would be much more effective to at least allow him partial entry before the speech starts so that he can hear the spoken warning. The entrance delay is not needed for the heat sensor since you would want immediate warning for a potential fire. The concept of the talking home security system can be carried as far as you have the incentive and potential funds to purchase alarm switches. Unfortunately, the major difficulty which arises in constructing such a powerful security system is the wiring of the windows and doors. An existing burglary system within the residence could be easily wired to your computer system in the same manner, thus saving you much toil and trouble. However, in most existing alarm systems, all switches are wired in series from window to window to door, thus precluding the identification of the place of entry. In that instance, your computer should speak "there is an intruder in the house." The resultant effect to the intruder would be the same once he has been identified.

A VOICE SECURITY LOCK

A very powerful use for a speaking computer system can arise if it is coupled with a simple voice recognition peripheral. Many of these devices are on the market today and this number will surely grow. As you add voice recognition to your speaking computer, you will find the possible uses for your system to become almost infinite. One possible rather farfetched use for a system that can be simply implemented would be a verbal security lock on your residence that would respond to preprogrammed voices.

Since most voice recognition systems have the capability for at least 16 input recognition phrases, they can be used in conjunction with a voice synthesizer to create a very secure voice-controlled lock system. The hardware configuration for this project is shown in Fig. 8-8. In addition to the speech synthesis peripheral, you will need a speech recognition system connected to your computer and some modifications to the entry door. First the door must be locked with an electronic latch that may be purchased at any home security system supply house. A single output bit from the computer is used to control the door latch solenoid through a power transistor suitable for the solenoid voltage. Also placed at the entry door is a pushbutton which will notify the computer of a desired entry, and a microphone and loudspeaker connected to the voice recognizer and synthesizer, respectively.

The operation of the system is determined totally by the software programming so there is tremendous flexibility for

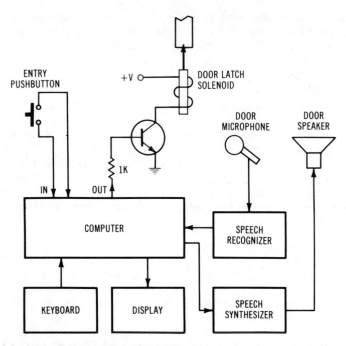

Fig. 8-8. A possible voice security lock system.

customizing the system to your own needs. However, let's look at a very basic operating program which might be used to control the voice lock system. This is shown in the flowchart of Fig. 8-9.

The real power of speech synthesis in this system is that the computer may request that the person desiring entry randomly speak one of four prestored words. The voice recognizer should be pretrained to respond to the same words. For instance, the recognizer might be trained to respond to the four words: hello, open, speech, and computer. The four words chosen should certainly be within the synthesizer's vocabulary, however. The speech recognizer is then trained to recognize the same four words from each person who is granted entry through the voice lock system. Upon computer command, the person desiring entry must repeat the word requested by the computer.

The advantage of this type of interactive system is that if a tape recording were made of your voice in an attempt to "fool" the voice lock system, the random choosing of passwords for entry

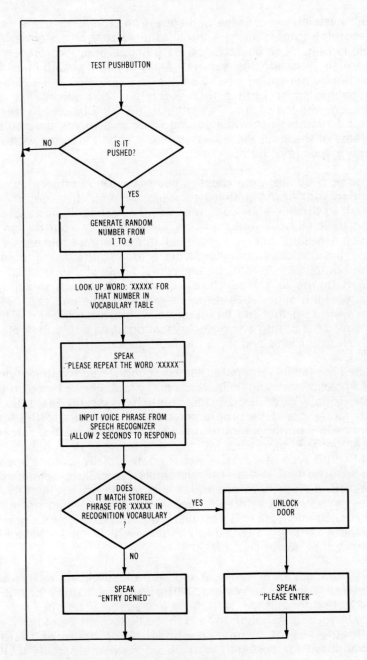

Fig. 8-9. A program flow for voice lock system.

will certainly discourage someone from trying to use a tape recording to gain entry. Although the voice lock system example is rather complicated for the ultimate end, it is presented here to illustrate the variety of application possibilities for computer generated speech synthesis. If you have the technical capability to go further, then you might start considering the implementation of speech synthesis in your kitchen to verbally "read" you recipes while you cook, or to give you a complete status of the household heating and cooling systems with the energy usage of both.

The possibilities are endless. If you have gone to the trouble of wiring your house systems to your computer, then you might want to provide your computer with the capability for answering the telephone and speaking. Depending on your design of such a system, a person could call home during a vacation trip, key in a few coded numbers from a Touch-Tone dial, and have the computer give a complete verbal home status readout on such things as temperature, security, number of telephone calls, etc. It might save someone much trouble and expense if he were told that the temperature within his refrigerator had risen to 80° during a two-week vacation, if he could then place a call to a friend and have the food saved.

Once the talking computer has been connected to a telephone, the possible uses again increase many fold. For instance, in the previously described home security system, the talking computer could be programmed to gain access to the telephone line during an intrusion, dial a friend (or the police), and then verbally report the incident and address in a request for help. This type of a system exists commercially, but the speaking portion of the alarm system is typically mechanically recorded and therefore relies on mechanical reliability. A computer with a synthetic speech peripheral would not have the mechanical reliability problem, but would, of course, need a standby battery power supply in the event of power failure or intentional power shut off.

So, there are some projects and possible applications for your speech synthesis system. Although the author has just scratched the surface with these few suggestions, they should spark your imagination toward those that might be directly applicable to you. Once you have your computer system configured for speaking with inputs from the outside world, you only have to write the software to bring your ideas to reality. The end results of hearing your system talk to you based upon events and occurrences can be quite thrilling.

Finally, as a last look at the applications for speech synthesizers, we must consider commercial uses. This is the arena in which the battles for superiority will be fought. As this book is being written, there are daily announcements of new inroads into markets with synthesized speech. Can you imagine walking up to a soft-drink vending machine and having it say, "Please insert 40 cents"?

Commercial Applications of Synthetic Speech

This is the area of speech technology that is running rampant. Manufacturers from vending machines to automobiles to children's toys are literally racing each other to produce the first integrated speech synthesizers in their products. There has probably not been such back lab hush-hush work performed in the American business place since the invention of the transistor. Everyone is trying to produce his products with the capability for speech, As this book goes to press, the following products have been successfully integrated with speech synthesis devices:

1. A talking clothes washing machine.
2. A talking microwave oven.
3. A talking soda pop vending machine.
4. A talking video arcade game.
5. A talking elevator.
6. A talking automobile.
7. A talking electronic multimeter.
8. Several talking children's hand-held electronic games.
9. Synthetic speech telephone directory assistance.
10. Synthetic speech airline flight information.
11. Synthetic speech stock brokerage information.
12. Talking clocks.
13. Talking televisions.
14. Talking calculators.
15. Talking language translators.
16. Talking phonographs.
17. Talking computers.

The list seems endless. In the next five or ten years the same list would probably fill four or five pages of this book. After all, the capability of providing a direct speech output to the user seems very attractive, but as our nation becomes more interested in bilingual education and language flexibility, which language will we use? *Written* text can be provided in two languages side by side for equal acceptance of either language. Multilanguage spoken text must be spoken serially, one after another. One of the problems which will be solved or ignored with the advent of talking products will be how do you speak the same phrase in many languages effectively? Maybe some day we might go down to the local department store to buy a microwave oven and be questioned as to whether we would like it in Spanish, English, Italian, or Hebrew? As ridiculous as that sounds, it will become, if it is not already, a serious question in the minds of marketers. Possibly the ultimate way to solve that problem would be to incorporate a language switch in universal products so that the purchaser could select the language of his choice. This appears to be the best way. It would provide a single universal product from each manufacturer.

At some time in the future we will all most likely look around us and question: "How long will the mute devices around us remain that way?" It seems only a matter of time until everything talks. Whether or not the talking items will be accepted by the public is up to us. The first few items in our home that begin to talk will surely be novel, but pity our grandchildren who will not be able to escape the electronic voices that surround them in the future.

This is by no means saying that the application of voice synthesis to any marketable product is bad. All it implies is that manufacturers must begin to think responsibly before they integrate speech into their systems. If we have volume controls and on/off switches to control what we hear, *and* we are still provided with visible displays, then we can have silence if we desire. Otherwise we might feel that we were continuously surrounded by crowds.

In closing this book on computer generated synthetic speech, let me remind you that you have just seen the tip of the iceberg. The science of generating artificial speech is still in its infancy. Indeed, some people *still* consider a talking computer to be in the realm of science fiction. By reading this book you have been given insight into the wave of the future. It is not science fiction, it is here. You have seen the voice of tomorrow.

appendix A
Glossary of Terms

ACATAPHASIA   A speech disorder with the inability to express one's thoughts.

ACOUSTIC   Relating to sound or hearing.

ADAM'S APPLE   Part of the larynx formed of cartilage, called the thyroid cartilage.

ADPCM   Adaptive Differential Pulse Code Modulation.

AFFRICATE   A consonant formed by the succession of two consonants such as j = D.ZH, resembles a fricative.

ALIASING   A condition or artifact occurring in signal sampling where a high frequency signal appears to be of lower frequency because of a low sample rate.

ALLOPHONE   Spoken variations of phonemes dependent on the phonemes and their placement within words.

ALVEOLAR   The gum ridge below the teeth.

AMPLITUDE	Magnitude, loudness, or volume of a signal.
ANALOG	Having capability of continuous variation without discrete discernible steps.
ANATOMIC	Pertaining to the structure of the body.
APHESIS	A speech defect characterized by the dropping of an unstressed initial vowel or syllable, i.e., example: zample; expect: spect.
APHONIA	Loss or absence of voice due to failure of vibration of the vocal cords.
ARTICULATE	To express orally.
ARTICULATION	A measure of speech intelligibility.
ARTIFACT	Something changed from its natural state by artificial means.
ARTIFICIAL	Produced by other than natural means such as artificial speech from synthesizers.
ASPIRATION	To breathe out during speech.
ATTENUATE	To decrease the amplitude or energy of a signal.
AUDITORY NERVE	The group of neurons passing signals from the ears to the brain.
AURAL	Relating to hearing and sound.
AUTO CORRELATION	A method of signal processing created by delaying the original signal and then multiplying the delayed signal by the original.
AXON	The conducting portion of a nerve cell.

B

BANDPASS — A filter allowing only a limited range of frequencies to pass.

BANDWIDTH — The important range of frequencies in a signal.

BASILAR MEMBRANE — Part of the inner ear which discerns frequencies.

BINARY — A number system with the base 2 with values of 0 or 1.

BIT — A single digit in the binary system

BROCA'S AREA — A portion of the brain in the frontal lobe which relates to language perception and expression.

BRONCHI — Part of the vocal tract excitation system extending from the lungs to the trachea (windpipe).

BYTE — A group of eight bits in sequential order.

C

CASCADE — Placed in series or sequence with each output feeding the next input.

CAVITY — A hollow area such as the throat or nasal cavity with associated resonances.

CEPSTRUM — The frequency spectrum of a frequency spectrum (an inside-out spelling of spectrum).

CHIRP — A wideband signal created by a rapid frequency sweep.

COCHLEA
The snail-like appearing part of the inner ear.

COGNATES
The related pairs of voiced and unvoiced fricative consonants.

CONCATENATE
To string together in sequence.

CONCHA
The part of the ear on which you hang your glasses, the outermost part.

CONNOTATION
The hidden meaning in a word or phrase.

CONSONANT
A speech sound in the category of a stop or plosive, fricative, nasal, liquid or glide, and semi-vowels; a nonvowel sound.

CONTINUANT
A static speech sound requiring no motion of the vocal tract other than the vocal cords and/or lungs.

CONTINUOUS SPEECH
Normal speech, without special pauses between words or unnatural emphasis.

CYCLE
A complete oscillation of a periodic happening or signal.

D

DAMPING
To cause a decrease in the amplitude of successive oscillations or cycles.

DECADE
The range of frequencies from one frequency to ten times that frequency.

DECIBEL (dB)
A quantitative unit of relative amplitude of two signals based on base 10 logarithms.

DELTA MODULATION
A type of digital encoding of an analog signal based on signal changes.

DIALECT

A difference in speech patterns caused by social or geographical differences.

DIGITAL

Relating to specific states such as binary as opposed to analog.

DIPHTHONG

A speech sound formed between two spoken vowels.

DISTAL

Away from the center of the body; toward the distant ends.

DISTORTION

Imperfections in the replication of a signal.

DYSPHONIA

An impairment of the larynx which affects proper voice production.

E

EFFECTOR CELLS

A nerve cell that acts as an output for the brain.

ELECTRICAL ANALOG

An electronic simulation of a physical occurrence.

ENCODING

Converting a signal from one form to another.

ENVELOPE

A description of the variation in the peak values in a time varying signal; the shape of the amplitude variations.

F

FFT (Fast Fourier Transform)

A means of mathematically finding the spectral content of a signal.

FEEDBACK

A controlled reaction in a system based on its output to reduce error.

FIDELITY

The accuracy of signal reproduction; lack of distortion.

FORMANT

A region of frequency prominence in the audio speech band; a speech resonant frequency.

FORMANT SYNTHESIS

A means of synthesizing speech based upon recreation of the formant frequency bands.

FREQUENCY

The number of occurrences in a given period of time (usually one second).

FRICATIVE

A speech sound consonant having a broad frequency spectrum, usually characterized by a hissing sound.

FUNDAMENTAL FREQUENCY

The lowest frequency in a harmonically distorted signal.

G

GA (General American) DIALECT

A standard method of characterizing English speech in America.

GLIDE

A speech sound consonant (in the category of semi-vowels) consisting of Y and W.

GLOTTAL

Referring to the slit-like orifice between the vocal cord lips.

GLOTTAL PULSE

The oscillation produced as air passes over the vibrating vocal cords.

GRAMMAR

Dealing with the formal features and use of a language.

H

HARDWARE

As opposed to software, the electronic components in a computer system and its peripherals.

HARMONICS

Distortions in a pure signal which

produce integral multiples of the fundamental frequency.

HOMOMORPHIC FILTER
A filter which passes a desired signal while rejecting all undesired components.

HOMONYMS
Words spelled differently but pronounced identically, i.e., too, two.

HYPERBOLE
A linguistic exaggeration, i.e., I'm *dead* tired.

HYPERURBANISM
An erroneous speech sound change made in an exaggerated effort to speak correctly.

I

IMPEDANCE
The apparent resistance of an electrical device to alternating current excitation.

INFLECTION
A means of "coloring" speech meanings with intentional pitch variations.

INSPIRATION
The pause in speech during which air is drawn into the lungs.

INTEGRATOR
An electronic circuit or system which performs a mathematical integration on a signal.

INTELLIGIBILITY
The clarity or understandability of speech.

INTENSITY
The loudness or amplitude of energy.

INTERPOLATE
To deduce internal quantities from the edge limits based on distance between limits.

INTONATION
Pitch changes in speech to express the importance of words or phrases.

205

L

LPC (Linear Predictive Coding)   A mathematical speech modeling method based upon digital filtering of voiced and unvoiced waveforms (parametric encoding).

LABIAL   Pertaining to the lips of the mouth.

LARYNX   The portion of the vocal tract in the throat containing the vocal cords.

LEXICON   A list of features of a language containing phonological, syntatic, and semantic features.

LINEAR   Moving along a line or continuous path as in an analog signal.

LINGUISTICS   The study of language.

LIQUID   A speech sound (also known as a semi-vowel) consisting of the consonants W and Y.

LITOTES   To strengthen the meaning of speech by a deliberate understatement, i.e., *not too bright* for *stupid*.

LOUDNESS   A perceived hearing sense based on sound intensity *and* pitch.

LOW-PASS   An electrical circuit which attenuates high frequencies and passes low frequencies.

M

MANDIBLE   The lower part of the movable jaw on the face.

MATATHESIS   The exchange of the positions of sounds in speech whether intentional or accidental, i.e., *ax* for *ask, flim* for *film, pervent* for *prevent*.

206

MICROPHONE	A mechanism for converting sound waves to electrical signals.
MICROPROCESSOR	The heart of a computer; the central processing unit (CPU) where decisions occur in a single integrated circuit.
MODULATION	A means of signal encoding; to impress one signal upon another.
MONOTONY	Having a boring pitch inflection or intonation.
MORPH	A sequence of concatenated phonemes which creates a minimal unit of grammar or syntax.
MORPHEME	The smallest grammatical unit which cannot be further subdivided, similar to a syllable.

N

NASAL	(1) Referring to the nose. (2) A group of speech sound consonants consisting of N, M, and NG.
NEURON	A nerve cell, the wires of the brain.
NOISE	A signal containing no information other than randomness; a wideband signal.
NORMALIZE	To scale a signal or quantity to a reference value maximum.
NOSE	The other part of your head which holds your glasses, also the place where nasal sounds exist.
NYQUIST THEORY	It states that to preserve fidelity, a signal must be sampled at least at twice its highest frequency component.

O

OCTAVE The range of frequencies from one frequency to twice that frequency.

ONOMATOPOEIA Use of a word to describe a sound, i.e., *boom* for an explosion, *tick-tock* for a clock sound.

OVERTONES Integral frequency distortion of a signal; harmonics.

P

PALATAL Pertaining to articulation with the tip of the tongue touching the roof of the mouth.

PARCOR Partial Correlation, a form of linear prediction of signals; a method of speech synthesis used by some Japanese manufacturers in their products.

PARSE To separate a phrase or computer program into the most elementary structural parts.

PHARYNX The throat from the esophagus to the mouth.

PHONEME The basic sound unit of speech.

PHONETICS The study of speech sounds and their production and perception.

PHYSIOLOGY The science of living organisms, their parts, and functions.

PITCH The predominant frequency sounded by an acoustic source.

PLOSIVE A speech sound consonant also known as a stop consonant.

PORT	A connection from a computer to its peripherals.
PROSODIC	Relating to the stress patterns of an utterance, normally longer than one word.
PSEUDORANDOM	Having the appearance of randomness over a limited period of time.

Q

QUANTIZATION	Converting from analog to digital or quantitative information.

R

RAM	Random Access Memory. Temporary read/write memory which holds data as long as power is on.
RANDOM	Equal probability of any occurrence.
RECEPTOR CELL	The input neurons for the brain.
RECONSTRUCTED SPEECH	Speech electronically regenerated from stored human speech.
RECTIFIER	An electronic element usually called a diode which allows current to flow only in one direction; used to convert alternating current (AC) to direct current (DC).
RECURSIVE FILTER	A filter with multiple feedback in a lattice configuration.
REFLECTION COEFFICIENT	A predictor value used for digital filtering in LPC speech synthesis.
RESONANCE	Having activity at a specific frequency while rejecting others.

RESONATOR | A mechanism which emphasizes certain frequencies over others.

ROM | Read Only Memory. A permanent computer memory normally used to store data or programs. The stored information remains with power off.

S

SEMANTICS | The study of word meanings as they are used.

SEMI-VOWEL | A group of consonant phonemes consisting of the sounds W and Y.

SINE WAVE | An oscillating analog waveform described by the equation: $\sin 2\pi ft$ where f is the frequency and t is time. ($\pi(PI) = 3.14159 \ldots$)

SLOPE OVERLOAD | An artifact of delta modulation which causes signal distortion; it occurs when the delta modulator cannot keep up with signal changes.

SPECTROGRAM | A plot of visible speech sometimes called a voice print; made on a machine called a spectrograph showing the frequencies of speech.

SPECTRUM | The complete description of all frequencies within a signal.

SPEECH SYNTHESIZER | The means for generating artificial human speech.

STOP CONSONANT | Also known as a plosive; speech sounds consisting of b, d, g, p, t, and k.

SYLLABLE | A segment of speech or writing longer than a phoneme but shorter than a word (except for single syllable words).

SYNTAX | The pattern or structure of word order in a phrase or sentence.

T

THRESHOLD | A fixed quantity or amplitude value used to select signals above or below that value.

TONGUE | The major speech muscle. The center of articulation.

TRACHEA | The windpipe from the lungs to the larynx.

U

UNVOICED | Speech generated without the use of vibrating vocal cords.

UTTERANCE | A spoken phrase or passage

V

VOCAL CORDS | The larynx which generates the glottal pulse excitation for voiced speech.

VOCODER | A shortened term for voice coder; any means for electronically coding speech.

VOICED SPEECH | Any speech generated with the glottal pulse excitation (vibrating vocal cords).

VOWEL | A speech sound other than a consonant. A voiced sound of which there are 12 in GA speech.

W

WAVEFORM | A general shape of an analog signal (as seen on an oscilloscope).

WHISPER

Human speech generated with totally unvoiced sounds.

WHITE NOISE

A completely random signal waveform that contains all frequencies; acoustically it sounds like a hiss.

appendix B
Advanced Readings

Physiology of Speech

R. Curry, *The Mechanism of the Human Voice*, David McKay Co., Inc., New York, 1940.

P. B. Denes and E. N. Pinson, *The Speech Chain*, Waverly Press, Inc., Baltimore, MD, 1963.

H. Fletcher, *Speech and Hearing in Communication*, Van Nostrand Co., Inc., Princeton, NJ, 1953.

G. W. Gray and C. M. Wise, *The Bases of Speech*, Harper & Brothers, New York, 1946.

H. M. Kaplan, *Anatomy and Physiology of Speech,* McGraw-Hill, New York, 1960.

W. R. Zemlin, *Speech and Hearing Science: Anatomy and Physiology*, Prentice-Hall, Inc., Englewood Cliffs, NJ, 1968.

Linguistics

N. Chomsky and M. Halle, *The Sound Pattern of English*, Harper and Row, Publishers, New York, 1968.

G. Fairbanks, *Voice and Articulation Drillbook*, Harper and Row, Publishers, New York, 1960.

Z. S. Harris, *Methods of Structural Linguistics*, University of Chicago Press, Chicago, 1951.

R. Heffner, *General Phonetics*, University of Wisconsin Press, Madison, 1950.

A. A. Hill, *Introduction to Linguistic Structures*, Harcourt, Brace and World, New York, 1958.

D. Jones, *The Phoneme: Its Nature and Use*, Heffer, Cambridge, U.K., 1950

J. Lyons, *Introduction to Theoretical Linguistics*, Cambridge University Press, Cambridge, U.K., 1968.

R. W. Shuy, *Discovering American Dialects,* National Council of Teachers of English, Urbana, IL, 1967.

Speech and Electronic Synthesis

J. L. Flanagan, *Speech Analysis, Synthesis and Perception,* 2nd Edition, Springer-Verlag, New York, 1972.

J. D. Markel and A. H. Gray, *Linear Prediction of Speech,* Springer-Verlag, New York, 1976.

A. V. Oppenheim and R. W. Schafer, *Digital Signal Processing,* Prentice-Hall, Inc., Englewood Cliffs, NJ, 1975.

A. Peled and B. Liu, *Digital Signal Processing, Theory, Design and Implementation,* John Wiley and Sons, New York, 1976.

R. K. Potter, G. A. Kopp, and H. G. Kopp, *Visible Speech,* Dover Publications, New York, 1966.

L. R. Rabiner and B. Gold, *Theory and Application of Digital Signal Processing,* Prentice-Hall, Inc., Englewood Cliffs, NJ, 1975.

L. R. Rabiner and R. W. Schafer, *Digital Processing of Speech Signals,* Prentice-Hall, Inc., Englewood Cliffs, NJ, 1978.

R. Steele, *Delta Modulation Systems,* Halsted Press, London, 1975.

E. R. Teja, *Teaching Your Computer to Talk,* Tab Books, Inc., Blue Ridge Summit, PA, 1981.

appendix C
Speech Synthesis Product Manufacturers

These companies represent a rather complete list of voice synthesis peripheral manufacturers.

Centigram Corp.
155A Moffett Park Dr.
Sunnyvale, CA 94086
(408) 734-3222

Cheaptalk; Alan Saville
P. O. Box 5190
San Diego, CA 92105

Computalker Consultants
Box 1951
Santa Monica, CA 90406
(213) 392-5230

Data Voice
2 North LaSalle St.
Suite 1900
Chicago, IL 60602
(312) 327-8488

General Instruments
600 West John St.
Hicksville, NY 11802
(516) 732-3107

Harris Semiconductor
Box 883
Melbourne, FL 32901
(305) 724-7407

Hitachi America, Ltd.
1800 Bering Dr.
San Jose, CA 95112
(408) 292-6404

Intel Corp.
3065 Bowers Ave.
Santa Clara, CA 95051

Interstate Electronics Corp.
Box 3117
Anaheim, CA 92803
(714) 635-7210

ITT Semiconductors
Box 749
Lawrence, MA 01841
(617) 688-1881

Kurzweil Computer
  Products, Inc.
33 Cambridge Parkway
Cambridge, MA 02142
(617) 864-4700

Master Specialties Co.
1640 Monrovia Ave.
Costa Mesa, CA 92627
(714) 642-2427

Micromint, Inc.
917 Midway
Woodmere, NY 11598
(516) 374-6793

Mimic Electronics Co.
Box 921
Acton, MA 01720

Mountain Hardware
300 Harvey Blvd.
Santa Cruz, CA 95060
(408) 429-8000

National Semiconductor Corp.
2900 Semiconductor Dr.
Santa Clara, CA 95051
(408) 737-5000 (Info)

NEC America Inc.
532 Broad Hollow Rd.
Melville, NY 11747
(516) 752-9700

Percom Data Company, Inc.
211 N. Kirby
Garland, TX 75042

Speech Technology Corp.
631 Wilshire Blvd.
Santa Monica, CA 90401
(213) 393-0101

Street Electronics Corp.
1140 Mark Ave.
Carpenteria, CA 93013
(714) 632-9950

Telesensory Speech Systems
3408 Hillview Ave.
P. O. Box 10099
Palo Alto, CA 94304
(415) 493-2626

Texas Instruments, Inc.
P. O. Box 6448
Midland, TX 79701
(915) 563-2171

Vodex/Votrax
500 Stephenson Highway
Troy, MI 48084
1-800-521-1350
(313) 588-0341

Voicetek
Box 388
Goleta, CA 93116
(805) 687-8608

appendix D
Speech Synthesis Applications Circuit Collection

This collection of speech synthesis circuits is "everyday working circuits." You may build them to be used separately or in conjunction with other speech synthesis circuits.

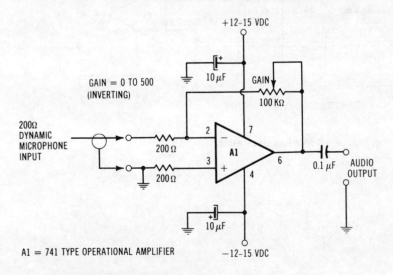

Fig. D-1. A dynamic microphone amplifier.

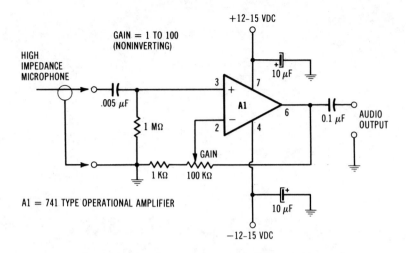

Fig. D-2. A high impedance microphone amplifier.

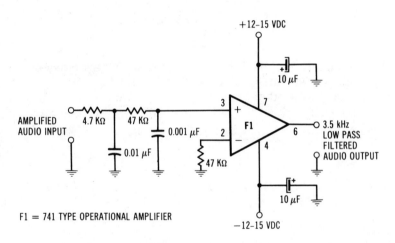

Fig. D-3. A 3.5 kHz low pass filter.

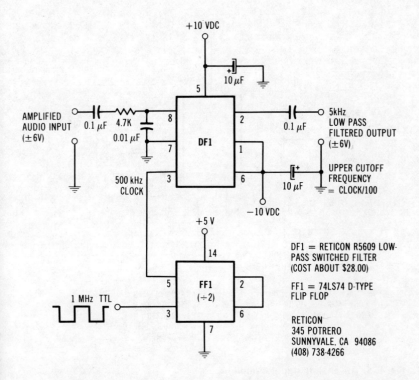

Fig. D-4. A 5 kHz super-fast cutoff low pass filter using switched capacitor filter.

219

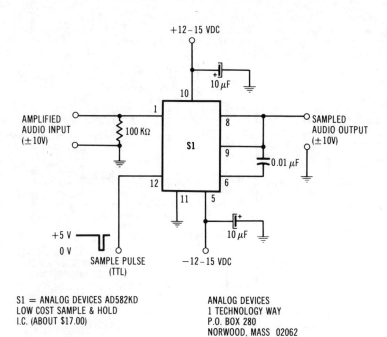

Fig. D-5. An analog signal sampler.

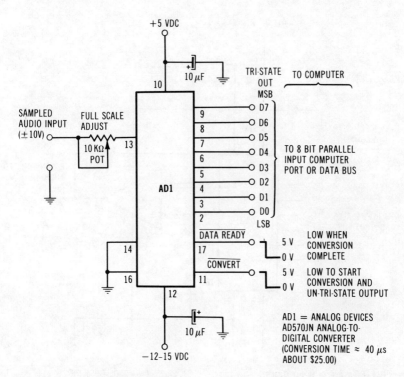

Fig. D-6. A voice digitizer circuit.

221

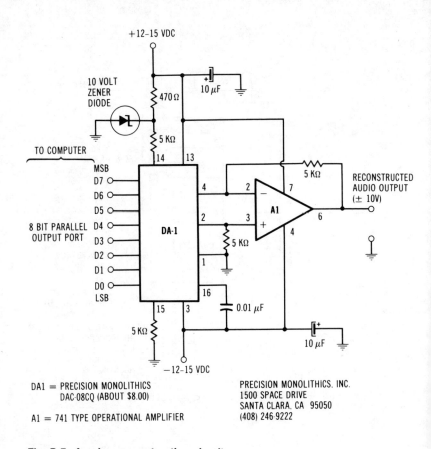

+12–15 VDC

10 VOLT ZENER DIODE

470 Ω

10 μF

5 KΩ

TO COMPUTER

MSB
D7
D6
D5
8 BIT PARALLEL   D4
OUTPUT PORT   D3
D2
D1
D0
LSB

14   13

DA-1

4   2

2   3

1

16

5 KΩ

A1

5 KΩ

RECONSTRUCTED
AUDIO OUTPUT
(± 10V)

7

6
4

5 KΩ

15   3

5 KΩ

0.01 μF

10 μF

−12–15 VDC

DA1 = PRECISION MONOLITHICS
        DAC-08CQ (ABOUT $8.00)

A1 = 741 TYPE OPERATIONAL AMPLIFIER

PRECISION MONOLITHICS. INC.
1500 SPACE DRIVE
SANTA CLARA. CA 95050
(408) 246-9222

Fig. D-7. A voice reconstruction circuit.

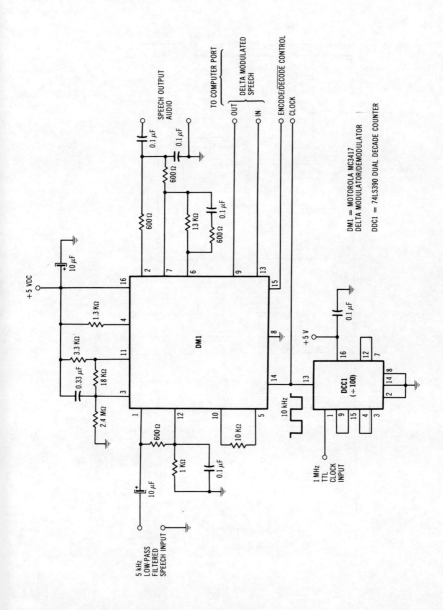

Fig. D-8. A delta modulation encoding/decoding circuit.

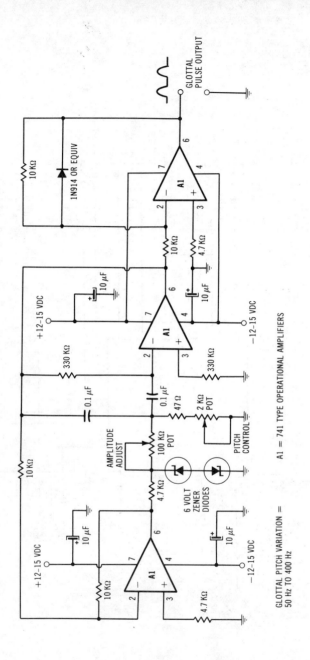

Fig. D-9. A variable pitch glottal pulse generator.

224

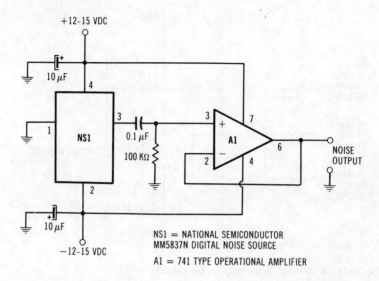

Fig. D-10. A digital fricative noise source.

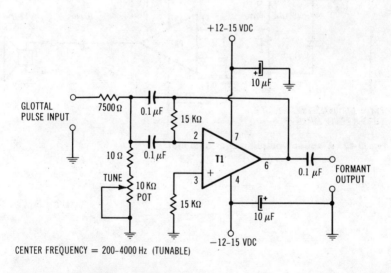

CENTER FREQUENCY = 200-4000 Hz (TUNABLE)

T1 = 741 TYPE OPERATIONAL AMPLIFIER

Fig. D-11. A tunable bandpass formant filter.

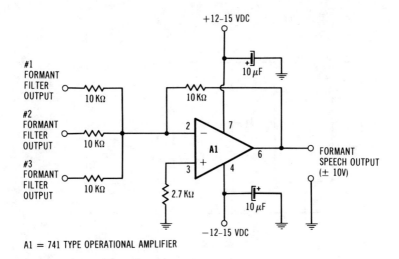

Fig. D-12. A formant frequency adder circuit.

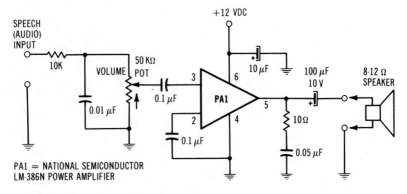

Fig. D-13. A speech output power amplifier.

INDEX

A

Applications
  aid to handicapped, 186-188
  commercial, 197-198
  lock, voice security, 193-196
  talking, a
    clock, 180-184
    doorbell, 189-190
    home security system, 190-193
Acoustic resonators, 72
Adaptive delta pcm, 100
Aid to handicapped, 186-188
Algorithm, text-to-speech, 157
Aliasing, 88, 199
Allomorphs, 50
Allophones, 43, 44, 106
Amplitude detector/threshold circuit, 63
Analog
  comparator, 96-97
  formant
    speech synthesizers, 146-161
    synthesis, 100-101, 128
      frequency, 14, 15-16
  integrator, 96-97
  -to-digital converter, 111
Annunciator precursor, 62
Articulation drill, 55-57
Artificial
  speech, 21
  voice, 18
ASCII, 165
Assembly language program(s), 93-94
Audio feedback, 25
Aural
  feedback, 24
  interaction, 63-64
    circuit, 65-66

B

Babbage's machine, 72
Bandpass filters, 15
BASIC, 43
Baud
  rates, 126, 159
  select switch, 159

C

Canned vocabulary, 125, 139

Chip
  speech synthesis, 173
  synthesizer, 152-153
    LPC, 166
CMOS techniques, 152
Cochlea, 27
Code generator, speech-to-LPC, 176-177
Commercial
  applications, 197-198
  uses, possible, 179
Compacted speech data, 129
Computer
  language, 43
  listening to, 145
  speech
    Cater's laws, 60-62
    courteous, 64
    interfacing, 59
    synthesizer, 19
Concatenate, 139, 151
  phoneme, 165
Converter
  analog-to-digital, 88, 89
  digital-to-analog, 114

D

Data
  frame, 106
    LPC, 113, 116
    types, 116-117
    unvoiced, 116
    voiced, 114
  rate, 126, 162
Delta modulation, 99-101, 135-137, 143
Demonstration number, 145, 172
Dialect, 57
  GA, 42
Diphthong (s), 43-44, 49, 105, 106
Digital
  -to-analog converter, 114
  vocal tract modeling
    of speech, 14, 16-17
    system, 18

E

Ear (s), 24-27
  listening, 54
Electronic filters, 33

Encoding
/reconstruction, waveform, 86
waveform, speech, 127
EPROM, on-board, 153

F

Feedback
audio, 25
speech, 25
Filters
bandpass, 15
voltage controlled, 38
low pass, 92-93
vocal, 32-38
audio, 33
electronic, 33
Flow of speech, 28
Formant
frequencies, 15-16, 34, 38, 72, 101-102
shapes of, 35
synthesizer, 103-111
analog, 79
FORTRAN, 43
Fourier synthesis, 119
Fricative, 25
phoneme, 47, 48
sounds, 31, 38, 73

G

General American (GA) dialect, 42, 44
Glide (s), 54
consonants, 47, 49
Glottal
pitch, 102, 103
pulse, 32, 33, 113

H

Hearing, 25-27
Home computer, 11, 16, 20, 90, 117, 118, 128, 145-146, 152, 157, 170, 179
interface, universal, 166
capability, storage, 82
synthesizers, speech, LPC, 164

I

Incremental encoding, 96
Integrator, 99-100
International Phonetic Association (IPA), 42, 45
Interface
converter, 174
module, 175-176

Interfacing, computer speech, 59

L

Larynx, 28, 29, 30, 31
Laser page printer, 13
Learning aid, children's, 17
Linear
predictive
coded, 16, 17
speech, 117
Linguistics, 39, 41-58
Lookup table program, 105
Low-pass filter, 92
LPC
devices, encoding, 119
technique, synthesis, 82, 84

M

Microprocessor(s), 121, 136-137, 166, 167-168, 173
controller, 159
input/output port, 143
internal, 165
on-board, 169-170, 171
self-contained, 157
6502, 176
Mechanisms, talking, 72-75
Morphemes, 50
Muscles, vocal cord, 30, 32
Most frequently spoken
sounds, 50, 52
words, 50, 51

N

Nasal consonants, 47, 48-49, 54
Nervous system, 23
Neurons, 23
Novelty uses, 19
Nyquist, Henry, 84
theorem, 88, 89

O

Optical
character recognition, 148, 149
tracking system, 149
nerve, 22-23
reader/speech synthesizer, 146

P

Parallel
ports, 171
computer, 156
data, 130
Parametric waveform
encoding, 123

Parametric waveform—cont
  synthesis, 126
PARCOR speech, 161, 162-164
PASCAL, 43
Partial autocorrelation (PARCOR), 16
Peripheral
  audio
    input, 67
    output, 67-69
Pharynx, 28, 29, 30
Phoneme (s), 15-16, 42-44, 46, 49, 52-54, 101
  continuant, 48, 106
  control tables, 109
  driven synthesizer, 42, 100-101, 105-109
    chip, 152-153
  major, 56
  noncontinuant, 106
Phonetic
  formant speech, 146
  synthesis technique, 82, 84
Phonology, 41
Pitch
  generator, 113
  voice, 32, 112
Place theory, 26-27
Plosive, 25
  sounds, 38
Port
  parallel, 143, 171
    computer, 156
    data, 130
Portable analysis and synthesis system, 176-177
Predictor coefficients, 117
Processor, speech, digital, 112
Pseudo-random noise generator, 113
Pulse code modulation, 89-90

R

Reading machine, talking, 18, 146-151
Real time speech encoder, 176-177
Receptor cells, 23
Reconstruction, speech, 78, 79, 80, 83-84
  mathematical, 79
Relative amplitude changes, 95
Resonance theory, 26
Resonated hiss, 38-39, 48
Resonator, 33-34
Riesz, R.R., 76-78
Robots, 11
ROM (s), on-chip, 162

S

Sampling
  absolute, 95
  an analog signal, 88
  mechanism, 85
  rate, 84, 86, 93, 106
  system, 88-89
  theorem, 88
Semi-vowel consonants, 47, 49
Sentence structure, 58
Software, 127, 129, 130, 157
Sound (s)
  consonant, 46-49
  effects, 94, 157
  fricative, 31, 103, 113
  nasal, 103
  power of, 53-54
  robotic, 103, 165
  voiced, 31, 103
  vowel, 44-46
Speaking bellows, 74
Spectrogram, 36-39
Speech
  artificial, 21
  direct waveform encoding/decoding, 139
  encoded, 111
  GA, 44
  generation organs, 28-32
  LPC, generation of, 173
  linear predictive coded, 162
  module, 156
    generator, 166-167, 169-170
  network, 22
  phonetic, 82
  production, 28
  rate, 130, 148
  recognition system, 67, 126, 145, 146
  reconstruction, 78, 79, 80, 83-84
  spectral content, 111
  samples, digitized, 111
  storage, 82-83, 130
  terminal, 123-125
  -to-LPC code generator, 176-177
  sounds, frequency of occurrence, 52
  synthesis
    basic methods of, 78, 80
      analog formant frequency, 101-110
      linear predictive coded, 111-119
      waveform encoding/reconstruction, 85-100

Speech—cont
  synthesis
    phonetic, 79
    tachometer, 81-83
  synthesized
    categories, 78
    types of, 79
  synthesizer
    articulation drill, 55-57
    interface, 130
    self-contained, 156-157
    waveform encoding, 127
Spooling, 63, 157
Stop consonants, 47-48
Synthetic speech, 12, 14
  applications, 180
  definition, 83-85
  delta modulated, 130
  products, 122
  true, 28
  system, minimum, 180
Synthesis
  Fourier, 119
  Walsh function, 119
Synthesizer (s)
  allophone, 109, 110
  analog formant, 146, 147
  LPC, 79, 164
  optical reader/speech, 146
  phoneme 15-16, 109-110
  speech, futuristic, 119
  text-to-speech, 151
  under test, 56
  vocal tract, digital, 161-167
  waveform encoding/reconstruction;
    129

T

Talking
  bellows, 73
  clock, 180-184
  doorbell, 189-90
  home security system, 190-193
  mechanisms, 72-75
  reading machine, 18, 146-151
Telephone theory, 26
Terminal, computer, 123-126
Test, speech synthesizer, 54-57
Text
  parsing program, 165
  -to-speech, 110, 165-166
    converter, 172-173
Theories, hearing, 26-27

TTL
  gates, 127
  parallel, 165
  ports, 151

U

Updating frame, 114

V

Verbal communication, 12
Vibration, glottal, 32-33
Vocabulary, 130, 132-133
  canned, 118
  custom, 119
  ROMs, 137-139, 140-141, 162
    custom, 139, 167
  self-contained, 157
  words, standard, 170
Vocal
  cord (s), 47
    muscles, 30, 32
  filters, 32-38
  organs,
    electrical, 75
    mechanical, 76
  tract, 20, 30, 32, 72, 116
    analog simulations of, 146
    envelope, 21
    memory, 21
    motion, 43
    positions, 44-46
    simulators, 13, 16
Voder synthesizer, 76-78
Voice
  print, 36-38
  security lock, 193-196
Voiced sounds, 31
von Kempelen, 72-74
Vowel sounds, 44-46

W

Walsh function synthesis, 119
Waveform
  coding, 82, 84
  encoded/reconstructed systems,
    122-123
  encoder, 79
  encoding/reconstruction, 14-15, 17,
    100
  technique, 86
Wheatstone bridge, 74
White noise, 30
Word list, 144

TO THE READER

Sams Computer books cover Fundamentals — Programming — Interfacing — Technology written to meet the needs of computer engineers, professionals, scientists, technicians, students, educators, business owners, personal computerists and home hobbyists.

Our Tradition is to meet your needs and in so doing we invite you to tell us what your needs and interests are by completing the following:

1. I need books on the following topics:

_____

_____

_____

_____

_____

_____

2. I have the following Sams titles:

_____

_____

_____

_____

_____

_____

3. My occupation is:

_____ Scientist, Engineer	_____ D P Professional
_____ Personal computerist	_____ Business owner
_____ Technician, Serviceman	_____ Computer store owner
_____ Educator	_____ Home hobbyist
_____ Student	Other _____
	_____

Name (print) _____

Address _____

City _____ State _____ Zip _____

Mail to: **Howard W. Sams & Co., Inc.**
   Marketing Dept. #CBS1/80
   4300 W. 62nd St., P.O. Box 7092
   Indianapolis, Indiana 46206

21947